BIRTH
OF A
NATION

ALSO BY AARON McGRUDER

A Right to Be Hostile: The Boondocks Treasury
Fresh for '01 . . . You Suckas: A Boondocks Collection
The Boondocks: Because I Know You Don't Read the Newspapers

ALSO BY KYLE BAKER

The Cowboy Wally Show
Undercover Genie
King David
Why I Hate Saturn
You Are Here

BIRTH OF A NATION

A COMIC NOVEL

Aaron McGruder and Reginald Hudlin

Illustrations by Kyle Baker

Three Rivers Press, New York

Published in the United States by Three Rivers Press, an imprint of the Crown Publishing Group, a division of Random House, Inc., New York.
www.crownpublishing.com

THREE RIVERS PRESS and the Tugboat design are registered trademarks of Random House, Inc.

Originally published in hardcover in the United States by Crown Publishers, a division of Random House, Inc., in 2004.

Library of Congress Cataloging-in-Publication Data is available upon request.

ISBN 1-4000-8316-8

Printed in the United States of America

10 9 8 7 6 5 4 3 2 1

First Paperback Edition

Introduction

GROWING UP IN EAST ST. LOUIS, I didn't realize how unusual the place was until I went away to college. I'd tell friends about my childhood experiences, and their slack jaws made me realize my hometown was different. I'd tell them about my family waking up with a hacking cough in the middle of the night because of illegal emissions from the local Monsanto plant, or the head of the school board hiring a hit man to kill the mayor, or the two nightclubs built side by side: Oz (for white people) and The Wiz (for black folk), or . . . hey, your mouth is hanging open too!

I mention this because a lot of things you will see in the book about East St. Louis really happened. There really was a garbage strike that went on so long that people put garbage bags on the roofs of their houses so packs of wild dogs wouldn't get into them. At one point, the city really was so broke the police department couldn't afford gas for patrol cars and cops had to make calls on pay phones because their walkie-talkies didn't work. A high-security fence really was stolen. Oh, I could go on and on, but enough about good ol' days. . . .

The positive side of growing up there was that I saw black people in positions of power managing their own city. I lived next door to the chief of the fire department. I went to the same school as the son of mayor of East St. Louis . . . sure it was a private school three towns over because the local schools were a mess, but hey, he was black man in charge!

Don't think East St. Louis has these problems just because black people run it. Sure, it's got a high homicide rate, but a lot of the dead bodies they find there were people killed in St. Louis, Missouri, then transported across state lines and dumped in "East Boogie."

For some reason, East St. Louis always attracted a certain unsavory "element." Before it even became a city, when it was just an island in the middle of Mississippi River, pirates would hide stolen goods there. It was also a popular location for duels, since it was between Missouri and Illinois and not under the legal jurisdiction of either state.

Later the U.S. Army Corps of Engineers dammed one side of the island and joined it to the Illinois side. With buried treasure and the blood of pirates, East St. Louis was born. Being that it was the first stop on the train after you crossed the Mason-Dixon Line, there were always plenty of black folks living in the city, happy to work in the factories or slaughterhouses.

East St. Louis evolved into a popular little hot spot. Before "Take the 'A' Train," Duke Ellington's theme song was "East St. Louis Toodle-oo." Miles Davis was born there; Chuck Berry and Ike and Tina Turner created rock and roll in nightclubs there.

White folks ran the city back then, and they kept up appearances enough for East St. Louis to be named the country's "All-American City" in 1959. As the industries of the Rust Belt collapsed, and the white people left right after the jobs did, East St. Louis suffered the fate of its "sister cities" Gary and Newark and fell into economic ruin.

I know all this city history because my dad arranged for me to write a series of radio spots documenting the history of the city for a local station while I was in high school. I was also studying for my insurance license in case this whole movie thing didn't work out, but he supported my dreams enough to get me a job doing something "creative."

My dad's dream was to turn the city around, so he was involved in public service his whole life. In addition to running his insurance agency, he also was the president of the Chamber of Commerce, president of the local state community college, and president of the local Kiwanis Club; he served on endless boards, from Junior Achievement to Target 2000 (a target which, apparently, the city missed). He was asked to run for mayor, but he was such a straight arrow he knew his intolerance of payoffs and kickbacks made him wrong for a life in politics.

Somehow my dad never got cynical about the city despite being fully aware of the levels of corruption and incompetence around him. Like our hero Fred Fredricks, he always fought the good fight. You can't be around a man like that and not inherit his passion for social change. But realistically, how could anyone reverse the economic and political forces that were holding down East St. Louis?

The idea behind *Birth of a Nation* came together while hanging out at the San Diego Comic Book Convention with friend and collaborator Aaron McGruder. We were trying to come up with a movie idea that was funny and easy to sell. I suggested the idea of East St. Louis seceding and forming its own country.

BOOM. A weekend of intense brainstorming turned into a year of obsession, with Aaron balancing the demands of his daily comic strip with working on *Birth of a Nation*. I can't imagine that anyone reading this book doesn't know that Aaron isn't the creator of *The Boondocks,* one of the most brilliant comic strips of all time. Aaron and I share many of the same interests—the global realignment of black people, alternative fuel sources, late '80s hip hop. Anyway, passions, dreams, and personal experiences were poured into the draft. Aaron's gift for writing socio-political comedy haikus made full use of the larger canvas of a movie script. But when we finished we had a project that fans of our work would love, but no movie studio would make.

Rather than have it sit on shelf, waiting for Jay-Z to buy Paramount, we decided to publish it as a graphic novel. Aaron and I quickly agreed that Kyle Baker would be the perfect artist to bring the story to life. I had worked with Kyle before—a teleplay that he wrote for my anthology series *Cosmic Slop* won some cool awards—and I knew his storytelling skills and versatile art style would be invaluable in translating our script into a illustrated style that would appeal to both comic book snobs and first-time readers of the format.

I want to thank all the wonderful people in my life that made this book possible. My brothers Warrington and Christopher, my superhero mom, the always inspirational Alice Randall, my minister Eugene Rivers, my right hand Robert Otey, my agent Norman Aladjem, my managers Mark Schulman and Howard Klein, dope designer Art Sims, Chris Rock, Nelson George, Craig Preston, Pierre Paradise (yes that's his real name), Denys Cowan, Dwayne McDuffie, Byron Phillips, Jeff Turner, Shurie Williams, Jeffery Sachs for confirming my suspicions, my niece Dvora Vener and the gang at BWR, Stephen Barnes, my amazing literary agent Lydia Wills, Chris Jackson for getting the joke and fighting the fight . . . and most of all, my wonderful wife Chrisette.

Thanks for teaching me how to maintain optimism in the face of insurmountable odds, Dad. This book is dedicated to you.

WARRINGTON HUDLIN SR.

1922–1998

—Reginald Hudlin

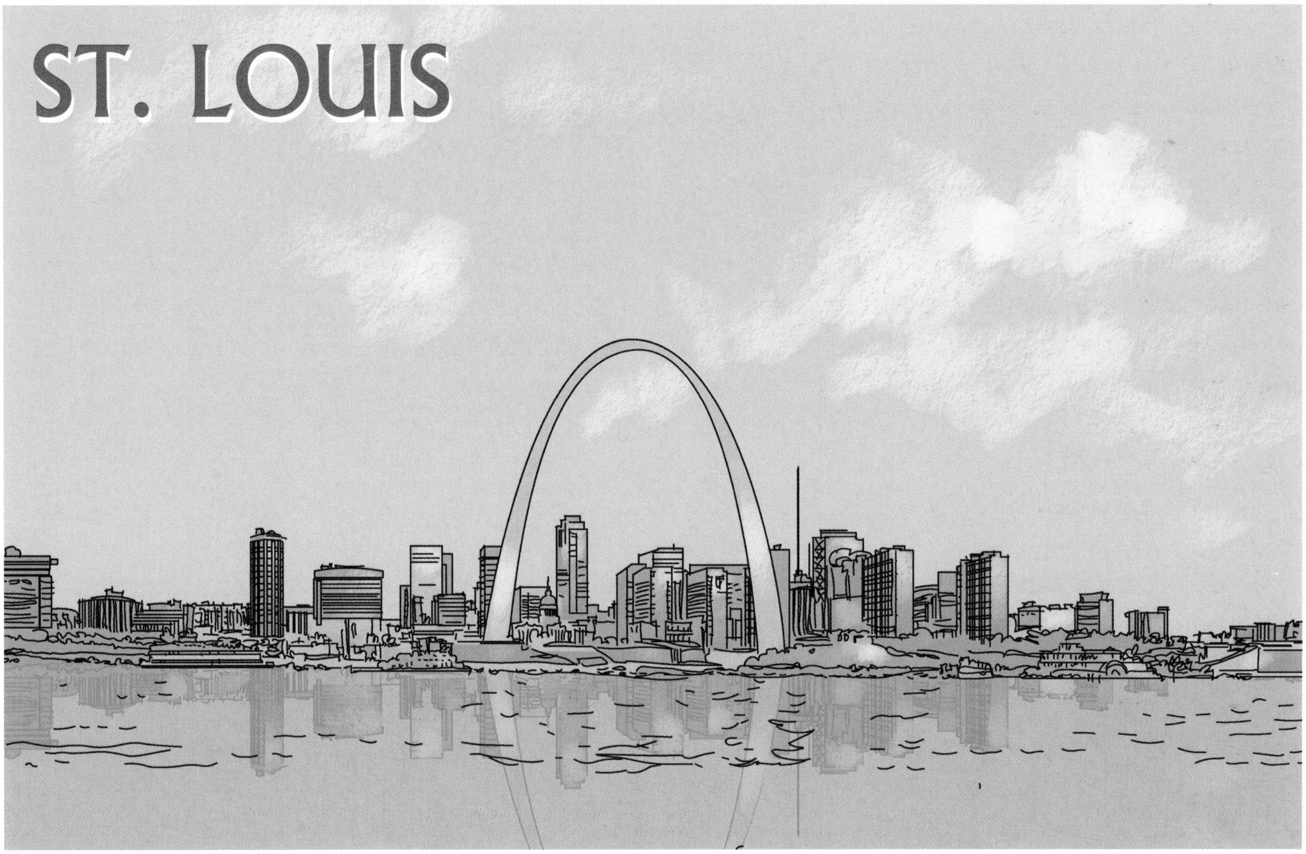
ST. LOUIS

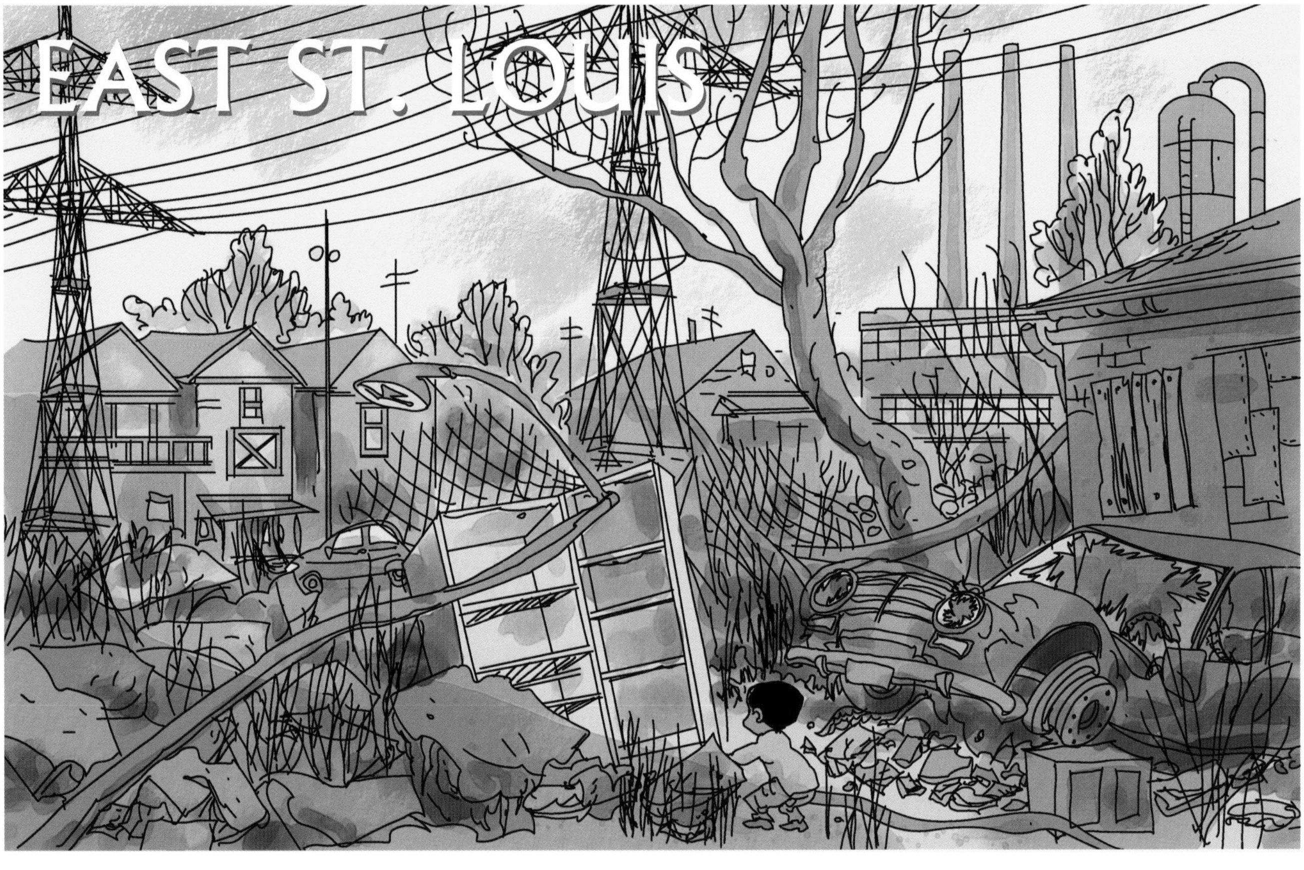
EAST ST. LOUIS

"....this is Tavis Smiley on NPR encouraging all of Black America to get out and vote today. We may not like the Vice President, but if Caldwell is elected...."

"Fred, do you think it's wrong to push up on a girl in Planned Parenthood?"

"Hold on, Kendrick— Ms. Jackson! C'mon now!"

"Now, just hear me out—I was there with Vanessa, right—we had a little ... accident, so, anyway, she wanted to get the morning-after thing—you know."

"What kind of 'accident'?"

"Hold on, Mayor. Ms. Jackson comin' ... I'm coming..."

"Huh?"

"What kind of 'accident'? Did the condom break?"

"Well, not really. We just both got twisted and forgot to use one, but that's not really relevant—"

"That's no accident. You were just irresponsible."

2

"Well I accidentally forgot to pull out before I—"

"All right, all right ... later."

"Beautiful day, isn't it, Ms. Jackson! Yessir!" He inhales deeply. "You smell that?"

"You mean the trash?" she answers. "Naw baby, Ms. Jackson been havin' trouble with my sinuses."

"That ain't trash. It's freedom."

"Another CNN–Time Warner poll says that 15 percent of people who support Governor Caldwell are reconsidering after his comments last week about Senator Clinton, putting him in a virtual dead heat with Vice-President Holden."

"God, that Hillary Clinton is such a beeyotch!"

"Does the red light mean it's on?"

Habib raps quietly to himself, "She don't know I'm cool as a fan, gat in hand, I don't want to blast her man . . ."

"Mayor Big Dawg!"   "Ha-bizib! What's happenin'?"

"Holdin' it down convenience-style, you know how 'Bib do. You ready?"   "Like Freddy! Hey, thanks again for letting us use the dumpsters during the strike."

"It's nothing. I'll see you at the King Elementary around eleven. To hell with Caldwell?"   "To hell with Caldwell!"

"Good Morning, Brother Mayor Fredericks, Brother Kendrick!"

"Mornin', Reverend!"

"And how are you this fine morning, Mr. Jefferson?"

"My yard smells like L'il Kim's ass crack after an hour on the StairMaster. How you think I am?"

"I heard that, Brotha Jefferson!"

"At least if I put it on the roof the dogs can't get to it."

"Good idea, Jefferson! Just be care—"

"See, that's an accident."

"Jefferson?! You okay?"

"So I ask myself, is it wrong for me to get her number? Does this constitute bad taste?"

"See you at the polls . . . to hell with Caldwell?"

"To hell with both them worthless ass-crackers!"

"Brotha Jefferson!"

"Oh shut ya ass, Reverend! I know you hear me, goddammit! I curse when I wanna curse . . ."

5

"I mean, on the one hand—nobody knows what she's doing in Planned Parenthood which admittedly a bit unnerving—"

"Hey, you listening, Brother Mayor?"

"I ask your opinion because I respect you as a moral leader."

"What do y'all ignorant niggas know about E-lectoral politics, anyway?"

"He's right, you know. It's a sham. Holden ain't no different from Caldwell anyway. Same shit, different toilet."

"MAYOR!!!"

"What's happening, Fred?"

"Y'all fellas gonna vote, right?"

"And you know that! I'm bringin' m' barbecue sauce, too."

"I'mma see y'all two there, right?"

The guys shrug.

"Now fellas, c'mon. I ain't take the time to get y'all registered for you not to vote."

"But Clyde there said the system's all messed up, right, Clyde?"

"Hey, don't try and group me in wit'chall apathetic asses. I never said I wasn't gonna vote!"

"C'mon, now! We partyin' today! We got folks cookin', we got a DJ . . ."

"Yeah plus hoes. AKA's from University of St. Louis."

"Word . . .?"

"Oooh Wee! AKA's? Them the, uh, real light-skinned sorority gals, right?"

"Yup. The good yellow-thickness. By the way, do y'all see anything wrong with gettin' a girl's number in Planned Parenthood?"

"Chaunda!!" calls Fred, "Honey, you ready?!"

"Chaunda! What are you doing in—Honey, you know I gotta be at the polls by 11:30!"

"Damn, Fred! Can't I vote tomorrow?"

"How's it gonna look, Mayor's girlfriend won't even vote? The news is gonna be there, too."

"I get to be on TV?"

"But you the mayor! You wakin' me up saying I'm making you look bad, and you hauling all this shit around in your car! That ain't yo' job! And why you still got this minivan? We should be ridin' in a 'imojene!"

"Honey, I don't—"

"Good to see that education payin' off for you, Mayor."

"Whatever I can do to help."

MARTIN LUTHER KING JR. ELEMENTARY SCHOOL

"What's everyone doin' out here! I wanna see some votin' going on!"

"I mean . . . Just look at this turnout. Biggest turnout in two decades! This is a community that refuses to not be heard."

"Mayor Fred Fredericks, here to cast my vote for Vice-President Holden."

"How are you, Mayor? Just a second."

"Um . . . There's some kind of—"

"What . . . what is it?"

"It says here you're a . . . felon."

A bunch of people laugh.

Fred chuckles. "A felon! Wait a minute, now I've never committed a crime I got caught for!"

More laughter.

"I'm sorry, Mayor. I can't let you vote."

"Well, we'll get this straightened out. Y'all go ahead."

"I've been trying to reach you for an hour. This has been happening at the other polling spots."

"Felon! I ain't no felon, I'm a United States postal worker!"

"Hey, I'm 'bout to be a felon if you don't let me vote for one of these worthless crackers!"

"I—I'm sorry . . . I don't know what's going on."

"Damn! I knew this was a waste of time! We ain't no felons!"

"Well . . . I am."

"Everyone just calm down. I'm gonna get to the bottom of this."

". . . gonna be a situation. No, we need County, no local cops. . ."

"I'm sorry, Ms. Jackson."

"I can't vote? Ms. Jackson can't vote?"

"Are you for real?!"

"I am for real!" answers the volunteer. The crowd protests loudly.

"Hold on, everyone just calm down. There ain't gonna be no trouble. I'm not going anywhere until I figure out what's going on!"

"Mayor, you and whoever else is on the list of convicted felons will have to leave and take this up with the elections board—"

"No, no . . . that'll take weeks to get straightened out."

"I'm not going to ask you again, Mayor."

"Wait . . . how you gonna tell him to leave —he's the mayor!"

"The federal government has jurisdiction here. You will leave or be arrested."

"We will not be moved."

"In the end, it came down to a single state, and with Illinois now reporting a victory for Caldwell by just under three hundred votes, we are ready to call it— Governor Caldwell of Texas, the next President of the United States."

"You did it! The American People did it! It was a hard fight."

"Some say this race has divided America. But I believe this spirited competition has brought out the best in our democracy—"

"So now it's time for a new era of bipartisanship. A new era of inclusion and understanding."

"For as I stand humbly before you all, I know that God has blessed this nation, and I will do my best to serve every one of its citizens."

CLANG!!   "God Bless America."

14

"This is the drama of a nation torn within itself," says Ted Koppel.

"A tragedy of errors—1,023 men and women, all black, from the virtually all black town of East St. Louis, prevented from voting by a private corporation charged by the State Government to purge the voter rolls of felons. A standard procedure which created a nonstandard constitutional train-wreck when 90% of the people removed had never actually committed a crime.

"It's the kind of glitch that can happen in a system as complex as ours. The kind of glitch that goes unnoticed, except when the race is decided by a single state, the margin of victory over Vice-President Holden, after three recounts, 157 votes. Now, as President-Elect Caldwell moves forward with his transition, the opposition leader Fred Fredericks—a small-town mayor of one of the most impoverished cities in America—crusades for justice. The Supreme Court has promised a decision later today in the case of the city of East St. Louis vs. Caldwell. At stake, the very soul of a nation. We'll be back with our continuing coverage after this."

JANUARY 5: A CONSTITUTIONAL CRISIS

"It's like someone breaking into your house, stealing your television, then when you ask for your television back, they tell you to get over it," says Al Sharpton.

The crowd applauds.

"Then they gonna make you watch the TV, but they hold the remote control. Now you gotta watch what they want you to watch, and it's your TV!"

A man in the crowd yells, "That's my got-damn TV!!!"

Sharpton's voice rises. "And they tell you to 'get over it.' Well I'm here to tell that fake President Caldwell that I can get over a lot of things, but I'm like Frankie Beverly and Maze, 'I can't get over you'!"

The audience screams. Al hands off the bullhorn to Mayor Fredericks. The audience calms.

"It's been a long fight. Lot of court battles, lotta marches . . ."   "I ain't tired!"

"Ain't nobody fixin' to go to bed!"   "Might go on longer . . ."

"I ain't tired! I bet' not see a tired nigga!"   "You see a tired nigga, you smack a tired nigga!!"

"Y'all ain't tired? I'm tired. Feels like quittin' time to me . . ."   The crowd yells at him not to quit.

"It's gettin' cold, too. You cold? . . . I gotta go, I'm going home."   The crowd screams, "No."

"What's that?"   The crowd continues to yell that he should stay.

"You mean . . . I shouldn't go nowhere? I should stay right here until I get justice?"   The crowd yells in affirmation.

"You sayin'—you sayin' I need to stay here so I don't let Ms. Jackson down?!"   The crowd screams its agreement.

"You said 'cause—'cause of Martin Luther King, and all the brothers and sisters who died for the Voting Rights Act of 1965? I should stay?!"

The crowd screams louder.

"Hold on! Wait a minute! Did somebody say I should stay because . . . What was that . . .? Something about Nelson Mandela saying one man one vote?!!"

The crowd is reaching fever pitch.

"HOLD ON!! If y'all saying what I think ya'll saying, then I need to stay because Patrick Henry said FREEDOM OR DEATH!!"

The crowd explodes.

"So I guess until we get our right to vote, ain't goin' nowhere, huh?! We ain't goin' nowhere!"

The crowd immediately joins in. "WE AIN'T GOIN' NOWHERE! WE AIN'T GOIN' NOWHERE! WE CAN'T BE STOPPED NOW, 'CAUSE IT'S FREEDOM OR DEATH!!"

"Oh no!! P-Diddy! I'm feelin' it!!"

"Ideology, organization, and action. When these elements are in place in the right order, movements form and thrive, like we saw in the Battle of Algiers. When they are not, movements fall apart."

"Kabilah, the decision came down!"

"Again, we will be going through this decision all day, but for now it looks like the Supreme Court has unanimously agreed that the people of East St. Louis were illegally disenfranchised."

"That is, their right to vote was unjustly taken from them."

". . . that their right to vote was unjustly taken from them!"

The crowd explodes again!

The reporter continues but can't be heard for several seconds because of the noise. "...too great a risk to the national stability to allow a re-vote that could overturn the results of this election, which they say would inevitably be contested in Congress and risk missing the constitutionally mandated deadline ..."

"...of the casting of electoral ballots. Again, it looks like the Supreme Court has ... with a five to four decision, denied a re-vote—"

A hush falls over the crowd.

"Call the N.A.P.P.'s. Tonight. My place."

"Well, I don't know about you, but I ain't leavin'! I demand justice!"

The crowd halfheartedly mutters, "Yeah ..."

"Y'all wanna ... sing, or something?"

"What do we do now?"

"Remember, Brother Fredericks, freedom is a road seldom traveled by the multitudes. We lost this one, but we'll keep fighting. You take care, Brother, I got a hair appointment."

"I'm sorry, Fred."

"Well, I got you. As long as a black man has a black woman to hold on to, he'll be OK."

"I'm leaving you."

"You can't be . . . This is a joke, right?"

"Nope. This shit is boring. Good luck with this whole . . . whatever . . . freedom . . . thing. I have to go get my back blown out now. Bye, Fred."

"The ballot or the goddamn bullet!!"

"Shush!! Not so loud, my daddy's asleep!"

"We can't sit by and let them get away with this systematic disenfranchisement of the black man! It's the ballot or the bul—"

" 'Ballot or the bullet,' 'Ballot or the bullet.' Will you give Malcolm X a rest, already? Every single meeting it's 'by any means necessary,' or it's 'chickens come home to roost' . . . I mean, if I take you to the bookstore, will you promise to buy another book?"

"His name, Nala, is Malik El Shabazz. Maybe you skipped the end of the book, but his name changed."

"Nala, Curtis ..."

"Hmm. Big words from a man who still goes by his slave name, *Curtis Martin.*"

"How you gonna talk about names, Nala! Like you ain't get yours from *The Lion King*! Disney—oohh, real progressive . . .'"

"Will you two cool it?! We are the New African People's Party! Mayor Fredericks needs our help! I want a plan, people!"

"Let's protest at the Supreme Court."

"I'm free Fridays and Tuesdays."

The rest of the group all starts talking at once. They each have one or two free days.

"This is why the white man keeps a foot in our collective asses! We never actually do anything!"

"Never do—What about our Kwanzaa Awareness Campaign?! Huh? We made people aware—of Kwanzaa!"

"Please! Kwanzaa's a stupid made-up holiday and it's never catching on! You know it, I know it!"

Everyone kinda nods.

"We have to do something for once! Look at us! We're too comfortable!"

"Hey—speak for yourself, I'm not comfortable."

Everyone voices their agreement.

"Here you go, guys. Be careful, they're hot ..."

"Thank you, Mrs. Randall."

"Mom ..."

"I'm sorry, Shannon— I mean, Kabilah."

"Hey, man . . . you did your best."

"What does it say about us, Kendrick?"

"What?"

"That we're gonna let them get away with this."

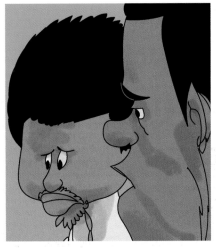  

"If they get away with this, we don't deserve freedom."

"Chaunda left me."

"Good. She wasn't right for you anyway."

"I loved her."

"Blah . . . She was action/adventure. Wrong genre."

"She was what?"

"Chaunda's action/adventure— She's an excitement junkie. You need romantic comedy."

"I can be action/ adventure!"

"Looky, every guy likes to think he's action/adventure. Deep down we all wanna be Han Solo. But we can't. Somebody has to be Obi Wan Kenobi."

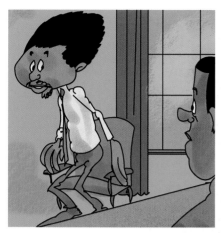

"What type of guy are you?"

"I holla at hoes in Planned Parenthood. If that ain't action/adventure, I don't know what is . . ."

"John Roberts is on the phone!"

"Oh, really? John?"

"You know John Roberts?!"

"We went to school together."

"Hey, John—"

"How you holdin' up, Fred? That was a hell of a beating you got yesterday."

"America got a beating yesterday."

"I got something important to talk to you about. You got dinner plans?"

"No."

"I'll see you in five hours. Oh, by the way—"

"Yeah."

"No snoot sandwiches."

25

"You two went to the same college?"   "Yep. Florida A&M."

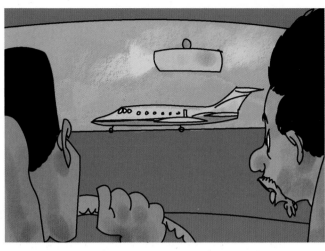

"Well, what classes were you taking if he ended up a billionaire and you pick up trash in 'the boogie'?"

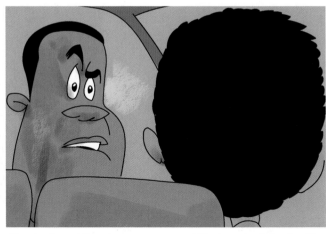

"So that's what a billionaire looks like in real life. My granddaddy said never trust the black man with no facial hair. Definite Tom."

"Louis Farrakhan has no facial fair."   "Yeah, ask Malcolm X about him."

"Jesus Lord, have—"

"—Mercy good God damn, what the Sam Hill . . .?"

"So what kind of movie is she?"

"Late-night Cinemax, I hope."

"You're gaining weight . . ."

"Only in the pockets, big boy. Fred, I'd like you to meet Donna Kelly."

"You know, my mother wants me to marry you."

"I'm sorry it's just— She's so impressed with your courage. I am too. I think all of America owes you a huge debt."

"Jeez! Women meet you, they ask for marriage. They meet me, all they want is stock options. So talk to me, Fred, what's the status?"

"The country is in trouble, that's the status."

"You know, my daddy used to say that trouble is just opportunity in work-clothes . . ."

"It won't work—Not in a million years. It's so incredibly insane."

"That's what they said when I started my network. That's what they said when I bought my airline—"

"Spare me the motivational speech, John. It's treason—"

"Fred, this ain't just a once-in-a-lifetime opportunity. This is a once-ever opportunity."

"To use me and use these people to make a buck? And maybe get us all killed in the process."

"Make a buck? Fred, my net worth is 1.2 billion dollars. This is about—"

"Black people get money, we're happy with a Bentley and a yacht. White men, they're not satisfied until they control their whole environment, and they'll risk everything to do it. That's why they run the world."

"Look, three days ago I was running one of the biggest record labels in the country. John's right. Even if we needed more money there are easier ways to make it. Our motives may not be the same as yours, Fred. But they're not at odds either."

28

"Fred, we can win. We can win big. But you can't be scared."

"I don't think he's scared, John. I just don't think he trusts us."

"I feel like I'm in a bad heist flick being talked into 'one last score.' "

"What do you need from me?"

"Let us start building the bank."

Fred nods solemnly.

"You know why we're going to win? Because they'll underestimate us. That's the one constant in business. We're all the same to them—a bunch of dumb country niggas. And every time, they underestimate me. And every time they do, I make 'em pay."

"I gotta return to New York tonight. Donna and I will be back here on Monday and we can get started."

"We won't let you down, Fred."

"What have I done?"

"I finally figured it out. She's a suspense/thriller. Lucky for you."

"Don't people get murdered in suspense/thrillers?"

"Yeah, but they usually get to have sex with the killer bitch before they die —so you're straight."

FEBRUARY 3

"Morning, Habib."

"Wow . . .what's wrong with you?"

"Could you make a decision, knowing it was the right thing to do, even if it might get you killed?"

"I can only hope that I would. But, more importantly, I know you would, my friend. That is what makes you a leader of men."

"... and who has been surprisingly silent since the Supreme Court decision a month ago, has scheduled an emergency press conference, which is set to begin any minute now—"

"Above everything else, keep it sincere. You're doing the right thing ... for your people."

"History will say we nearly slept."

"Thousands of Americans had the right to vote taken from them. Yes, they were poor black Americans, but they were Americans. They sought refuge in the law. They trusted the courts. But they did not find justice."

"Eventually, we were supposed forget that the man who got the least votes won the Presidency. Eventually, the nagging voice in the back of our minds telling us that we don't really live in a democracy anymore would fade into nothing. Eventually, we'd be able to look in the mirror and not feel guilty that we didn't do something."

"Before there was a Constitution to bicker about, there was this. The Declaration of Independence. It says two very important things. It says no taxation without representation. . ."

". . . and it says when the government no longer respects the freedoms of the people, the people have an obligation to not let it slide. It's not your choice, or even your privilege—it's your duty to fight back."

"History will say we almost failed that duty. Almost, but not quite."

Click

"Does this guy ever stop bitchin'?"

"I'm sorry, Captain, were you watching that? Hey . . . isn't that your home town?"

"You know it is, sir. I'd like to see it."

"And I'd like to see me care, boy."

"Don't let these stop you, boy."

"See I know the job of defending freedom ain't an easy one. But it's a job, and like any other job, you gotta get outta bed and do it whether you want to or not."

"I do hereby dissolve all political bonds between the city of East St. Louis and the government of the United States of America. We will create a new nation and chart our own destiny, as the forefathers of this country did when their freedom was threatened. And history will say Americans never forgot the true meaning of liberty. Thank you."

"Holy shit!!"

The room explodes with questions and camera flashes.

"My God, that was perfect!"

"Way to go, Mr. President."

Fred faints.

"...in absolute shock. None of us in the news business, it's safe to say, has seen anything like this before. Former Vice-President Holden has just released a statement he had no involvement in this . . . again, the city of East St. Louis has, according to its mayor, left the United States of America—"

"So, they succeeded?!"

"Now, they haven't succeeded at anything yet."

"They broke away
from the Union?"

"Well, it appears that's what they've done, but
whether or not they succeed is up to us."

"How can their succeeding
be up to us when you said
they just did it?"

"No, I said they
haven't succeeded,
haven't—

"What
the . . . ?"

"Sir, I believe the
word you're looking
for is 'secede.'"

"Isn't that
what I
said?
Succeed?"

"No sir—You're saying suc-ceed, with a hard 'C'—as
in 'to achieve.' To leave the union is to se-CEDE. While
they have apparently seceded, they have not
necessarily succeeded in whatever . . . they hope to
accomplish."

"I say we hang
every last one
of those
treasonous
bastards!"

"The first thing we need
to do is move the National
Guard in to secure the city
until we determine what
exactly is going on."

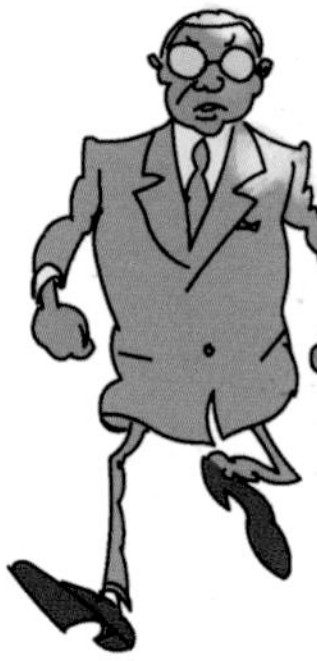

"Sir, I apologize for being late. And that is exactly what we do not need to do."

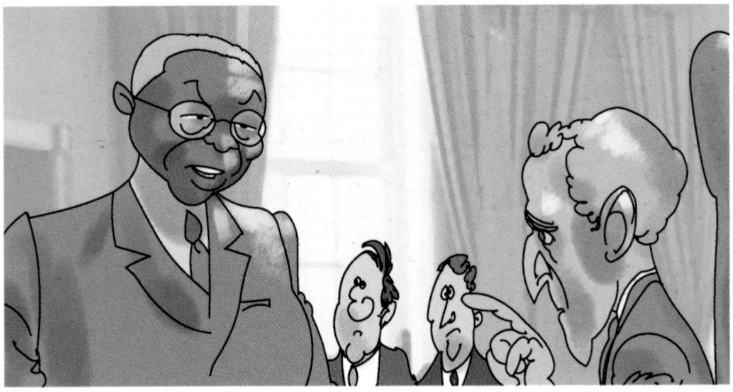

"First of all, I wouldn't send the National Guard on a mission to secure a puppy turd. Understand what's at stake, gentlemen. Maybe the country, but definitely this administration."

"Yes . . . yes . . . The ball rests squarely on our shoulders."

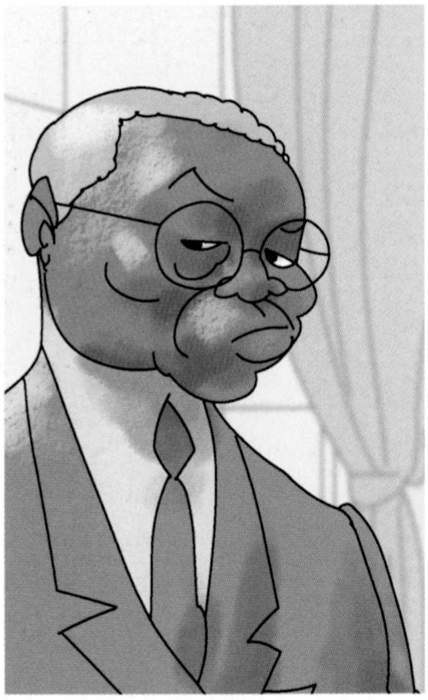

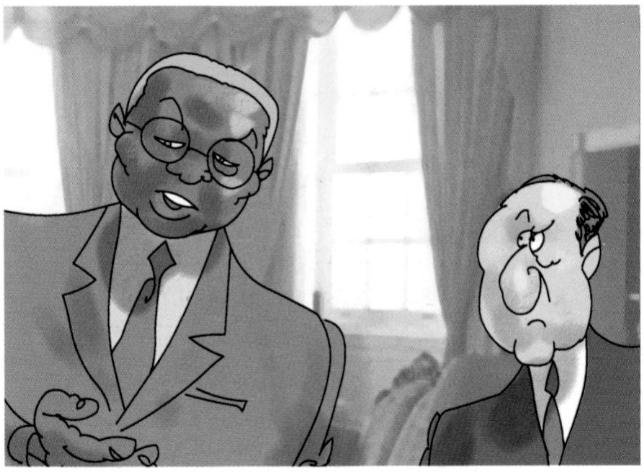

"Uh, right, Mr. President. And remember, this isn't a bunch of Branch Davidians in Waco. It's old black grandmothers who just wanted to vote. If people, anyone, started dying . . ."

"Suddenly we're the redcoats."

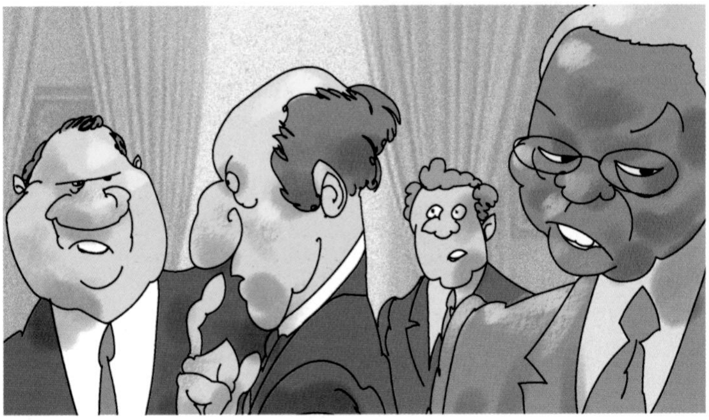

"The fallout would be Waco times a thousand."

"Wait . . . you think that could be the plan here, to lure us into an attack—"

"The fallout of which would end this administration."

"I don't know. It's possible. I'm just saying—"

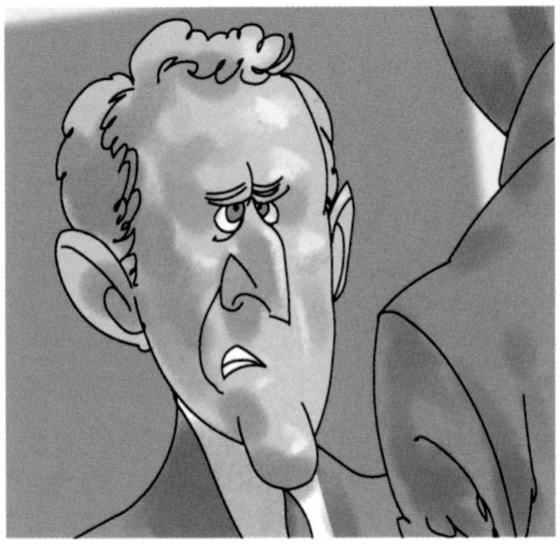

"You're saying we don't want to screw ourselves in the foot."

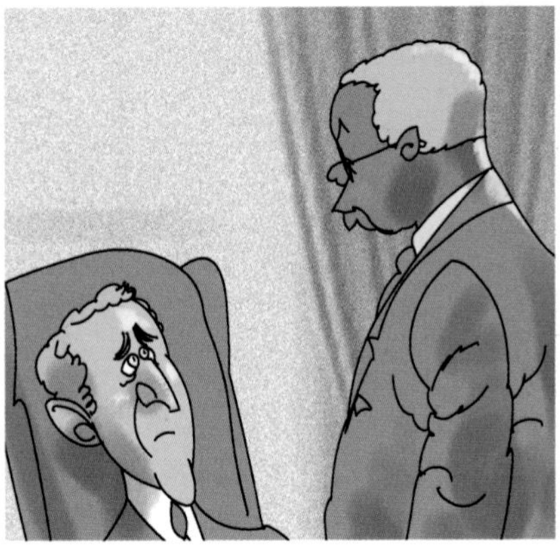

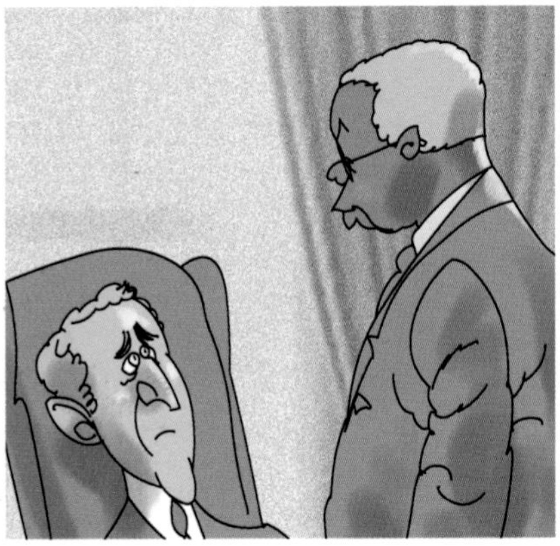

"Uh . . . precisely."

"So we do nothing while the Union falls apart? And what happens when Kansas City decides it wants to be part of Canada?"

"This isn't Kansas City. It isn't even St. Louis . . . it's East St. Louis. These people have nothing."

"East St. Louis: population 35,000, one of the most destitute towns in the United States."

"The air and the soil have been heavily contaminated by the local factories. In Illinois it ranks first in fetal death, first in premature birth, and third in infant death. It has one of the highest rates of asthma in the country . . ." She flips through pages. "Let me know when to stop. Let's see, the homicide rate is about 13 times higher than the norm for a city of its size."

"Jesus, what a shithole!"

"Literally. Sewage regularly floods homes and runs into the streets, no regular garbage pickup . . . It's a little slice of the third world right here at home. Unlivable by American standards. There isn't even a place to have a baby . . ."

"The whole damn city is dependent on the government, whether it's a government job or a welfare check. Cut them off and in two weeks they go away for an apology and a maternity ward."

"And reward them for treason?"

"Okay. We'll hold off on the Guard for right now. We'll show 'em what happens when you bite the shit that feeds you."

"This is such a proud day. All those in favor of an immediate journey to our new Black Homeland?"

"Right, see . . . check this out. Some of us should hold it down here, right? Like reserves, right? Cause we shouldn't all be at the same place at the same time . . ."

"Brothers and sisters, let's prepare to go to our new home."

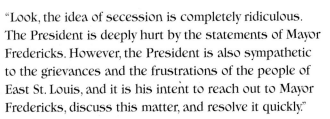

"Look, the idea of secession is completely ridiculous. The President is deeply hurt by the statements of Mayor Fredericks. However, the President is also sympathetic to the grievances and the frustrations of the people of East St. Louis, and it is his intent to reach out to Mayor Fredericks, discuss this matter, and resolve it quickly."

A barrage of questions. Something about the National Guard.

"No, the President has requested the National Guard not be deployed. He views this like a family disagreement and intends to work it out as a family."

"Fired?!"

"Until further notice. Just got the fax from the Postmaster General. Sorry folks. Viva la revolution."

"Fredericks!"

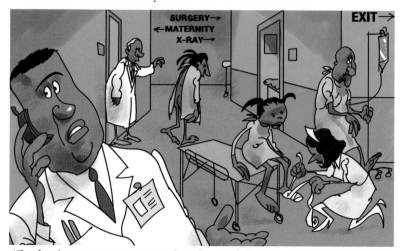

"Fred, what you want me to do? None of these people has health insurance—we didn't have enough money to operate before you—"

"A couple days to get things together . . . I'll get you the money you need. Please, Stan."

"Fred, I can give you till tomorrow. You don't come up with something by then, this hospital will shut down."

"Fred, I know you're upset..."

"It's not like we didn't know this was going to happen!"

"Fred..." "John promised me that by the time I gave the speech we would have enough money to operate. Now he's saying two weeks?!"

"There's been some delays with the bank, Fred."

"Delays. What kind of delays?"

"We've had three robberies this week alone. We just put up a fence with guard dogs. Why didn't you tell me this place had so much crime?"

"It's East St. Louis."

"Mr. Roberts, I've been trying to reach you all day, we've been robbed again!"

"*We've* been robbed? Well, I wasn't aware you were a partner in this venture. How much did *we* lose?"

"We lost— I mean, you lost—"

"And what happened to the fence and dogs around this site?"

"They stole the dogs— and the fence."

"They stole the . . . Jesus did they steal the security guards, too?"

"We think so, yes."

"I know who did this."

"He going to show?"

"Who knows?"

There are noises of people outside the room.

A secretary's voice is heard. "Wait . . . you can't just—"

"Roscoe."

"What's happenin,' Fred? Chaunda sends her regards."

"We called you in to talk about my property—"

"Is your name Fred? Huh? I'm talking to Fred right now."

"Now, Fred, first you niggaz come up in my backyard building this . . . whatever y'all are building. I got no calls, my people got no calls."

"I thought it was the city's land."

"And I thought I wasn't talking to your ass, chatterbox. I'ma call you chatterbox from now on."

"Hey! Roscoe, c'mon! Put the gun away!"

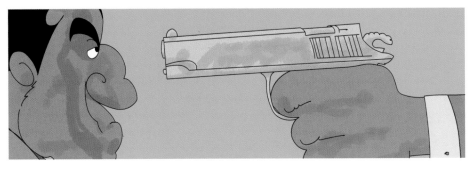

"So anyway, I turn on the television and found out y'all niggaz done went and started a new country. I mean, can you believe that?"

"I can't believe it, Roscoe. Hey, man, did they call you?"

"Naw, man . . . I got no call. Here I am . . . an icon of this community. So first, I wanna know what y'all are up to. Second, I wanna know why I shouldn't just take all this shit over myself right now."

"I'm waiting—"

". . . can see there looks to be a steady stream of cars leaving the city . . . a lot of us have been too stunned to take this seriously but a border is being set up . . . this thing appears to be for real. . ."

"Hey, babies. Welcome to East St. Louis. Now, Ms. Jackson's gonna have to see your passports."

"Oh my god, how cool is that? We have to show passports!"

"I'm sayin', gurl . . . what's up?"

"Dems yo' niggas?"

"Them?! Please."

"Now, Shannon—you sure you want to come in here? I mean . . . It's kind of a shithole."

"This is my cell. We don't know where we're staying yet."

"We're going."

"So you see, Roscoe, what we're doing here is complex. Pulling this off will require tremendous political savvy and expertise."

"I see . . . so it's politics."

"Yes. Politics. Very political. Now, most of the cops have already left the city. We'll need someone to keep the peace. You know any men who would like to get paid to stand around and hold guns all day?"

"I may know of such men . . ."

"Fred, can you keep him on a tight enough leash? 'Cause if not—"

"Look, I think working with him is a huge mistake, but I'll be waiting for an excuse to throw that societal shit stain in jail. Now what about the money?"

"We'll be operational in two weeks."

"Not good enough. People are leaving the city, if we—"

"Great. Less people to worry about."

"It's our job to take care of these people, John. You'll have to float the city until the bank opens."

"Is that right?"

"It's our only option; I'm not letting the hospital close."

"Fred's right, John. If everyone leaves the city before the bank is open, we got nothing."

"How many of these people are on welfare?"

"Seventy-five percent."

"Ain't this a bitch."

"Get a got-damn job! All of you!"

Fred tries to be heard, but everyone is yelling questions at once. Mostly about getting their checks.

"Need I remind y'all that we got a brand-new Church's Chicken downtown? You gonna mess up that progress with all this uppity foolishness, boy!"

"Listen, people, please. Let's not pretend like we haven't known tough times already. Heck, all we've known is tough times."

The crowd starts to calm.

49

"This city will have more money now than we've ever had. I promise you that on the 15th everyone will receive their regular government checks . . . Plus 100 bucks!"

The crowd reacts positively to that.

"And what the hell am I supposed to do? I'm out of a job now!"

The other government employees voice their concerns.

"Like we ain't gonna need mailmen, Brother Jefferson? We're in this together and we're going to win together. We've trusted them our whole lives, and look where it got us. Now we gotta trust ourselves."

"What's the name?"

"Excuse me?"

"Our name? What's the name of the new country? Ain't we got a name?"

"Well, Mrs. Carter. It's your country—what do you think the name should be?"

"Well . . . gee . . . um . . ."

"New Africa!"

The crowd explodes in argument over that name.

"Whoa, people! Easy! We'll figure out a name! I will form a committee where any and all loyal citizens shall meet to pick the name of our new land! We'll call it . . . the 'Nation Time' committee!"

"What's our flag gonna look like?"

"That's up to you!"

"Do we get our own national anthem?!"

"Join the committee and it's up to you, Brother Sam!"

It's like church now. Several people loudly volunteer.

"People of East St. Louis . . . It's Nation Time!!"

"YAY!!"
"YOU GO FRED!"

"Can I get my trash picked up?"

The crowd turns angry, complaining about the garbage.

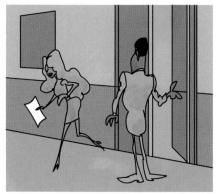

"Are you kidding, that was great! And the Nation Time thing? Inspired. Keep 'em—"

"Thanks . . . Poll numbers look great. 32% for, 28% against, 34% undecided. And it looks like we just got recognized by Cuba."

"What was I saying? Oh, the Nation Time thing. Smart. Keep 'em occupied. Great."

"I just thought the people should be involved as much as possible."

"Awww . . . you're so adorable."

"Ummhmm . . . 'President Pa-dussy.' Be careful with Roberts's girl."

"What, you think . . . Donna and Roberts?"

"If you had a billion dollars, wouldn't you hit that?"

"More popular than the President of the United States. That's what the polls are saying today about Fred Fredericks. Here's more:"

"All over the country, people are talking about Fred …"

"Y'know … I don't necessarily agree with his politics, but that Fred Fredericks is a true patriot."

"And, they're buying Fred …"

"Fred Fredericks! He is … um … how you say … hero! American hero!"

"They're even slamming for Fred."

"That last dunk there at the half there was pretty nasty. That one was for my man Fred Fredericks. Keep your head up, baby."

"Fred Mania is sweeping the nation—"

"The troops are gettin' awful restless. It looks bad, James. Bad."

"Sir we've discovered who's funding the situation in East St. Louis. We're moving to freeze his assets."

"Excellent work, Condice."

"Now me and the boys, we're stickin' with you. Tellin' folks to sit tight and you're fixin' to teach these uppity folks a thing or too when you're right good and ready. Just don't take too long."

"The good Christian people of Mississippi don't take too kindly to secession."

"So here's what we've decided. If you can stop crime, completely, in this city for twenty-four hours, than we'll make you our first general. Understood?"

BANG!

"You can't shoot anybody!"

"Hey, you never said we couldn't—" "Try again!"

"Move it! Everybody out, now!!"

"Eddie, is that you? Nigga, I bought crack from you last week!"

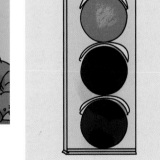

"Hey, man—you ain't never said we couldn't blow shit up."

"Try again!"

"God, I wish he'd stop smoking those damn cigars."

"This was your idea."

"It's a new day up in this bitch—Basically these streets belong to me—Roscoe . . . The General. General Roscoe, y'heard? We about to take it back to some ol' high school shit and start smackin' niggas in the face just for livin'."

"Um . . . Okay, well . . ."

"Fred, the White House just called for the fifth time today. They're insisting they send someone over immediately to negotiate."

"We can't stall them forever."

"Tell them we'll only talk to the Secretary of State. They'll never send him."

"Why not?"

"The Secretary of State oversees foreign affairs. If he comes it would look like they're recognizing us as a separate country."

"It'll buy us time."

"What's the status on those checks?"

"City treasury says Roberts hasn't given them the money yet. I'll go look for him now."

"So look, man. We got our own country now . . . You the . . . emperor or whatever. You make the rules. You know where I'm going with this?"

"Where, Kendrick?"

"Harems. Now hear me out. I've been reading about this."

"Now if you're like me, you like brown, yellow, Puerto Rican, and Haitian, so I got these brochures. Now immigration laws prevent bringing these women here without marrying them—but . . . heh, heh . . . we don't have to worry about that anymore, do we . . ."

"Kendrick, if I've got a harem of women from all over the planet, how does any work get done?"

"Oh, that's easy. You just keep Jesus first, homie. Everything else will fall into place."

FEBRUARY 18

"Good evening, friend."

"Omar. I dared to hope I'd never see your face again."

"Your homeland calls upon you once again, my friend."

"This flag comes with a generous donation from Nike."

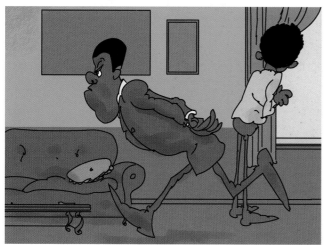

"Jesus, where are Donna and Roberts?"

"Niggas is mad . . . You better give 'em they money."   "She's here."   "C'mon . . . It's time!"

"Where's Roberts?! You see what's going on outside?"   "Come on!"

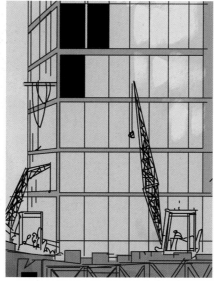

"John, we're gonna have a riot if we don't get people their checks."   "I know."

"Why haven't you put the money in the treasury!?"   "There is no money. The government froze all my accounts two days ago. Over a billion dollars. Gone."

"Shit. So What are we going to—"

"We opened for business twenty minutes ago."

"And . . .?"

"And we just made half a million dollars!"

"So I don't get it . . . What's the big friggin' deal about a bank?"

"I'm trying to tell you it's not an ordinary bank. Now it all makes sense. All of it—"

"Jesus, what? And keep it simple— don't talk a hole in the ground."

"Sir, Fred Fredericks and John Roberts have opened an 'offshore' bank, only it's not offshore."

"You've heard of Swiss Bank or Cayman Island accounts? I mean, you're from a wealthy family, so—"

"Okay, this morning around 9:15 we picked up a flood of financial traffic all over the world. Lots of money moving, and all to the same place. East St. Louis."

"Okay, okay . . ." says the President.

Condice continues, "The money is being transferred to a bank they've opened. Now, what makes this bank special is that it uses a series of personal identification numbers and passcodes instead of names. It's completely anonymous. Very attractive to people who make large amounts of money but don't want their government to know. Arms dealers, drug lords, divorcees— In exchange for this anonymity, these banks usually charge a fee. A few percentage points. Nothing compared to the money investors stand to make. And with the bank located within the continental United States, the currency exchange happens quicker, so what happens is—"

"So what does this mean?"

"With that much money, not only are they a real threat to National Security, but it could set off chain-reaction secessions—"

"How much money are they going to make anyway?" asks the President.

"They'll be the richest nation in the world, per capita, in approximately nine months."

"Nine months?"   "Give or take a month."

"Don't you ever knock?"   "Sir, I have the . . . OPEC Ambassador to see you."

"Send him in."

"Habib!"   "President Big Dawg!"

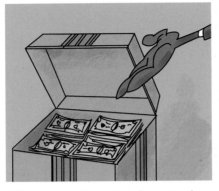

"They made you Ambassador?!"

"That's nothing—I'm here to present you with a gift from the coalition of OPEC nations."

"They hope this initial deposit of 20 million dollars will serve as a symbol of our hopes for a productive and prosperous relationship between our nations."

"Plus I'ma hook you up with a free Slurpie, dawg."

"Still think this is 'all just gonna go away,' Jack? Huh?!"

"Well, let's just see if it's 'all going away.'"

". . . being told now now that they may have to close the border to East St. Louis until they can figure out what to do with all of these new 'immigrants,' so to speak, people seeking to take advantage of the small city-state's newfound wealth."

"We underestimated them."

"You underestimated them, Jack! You!"

"We're weathering the storm. The President's approval rating is ten points higher than when this all started."

" 'Both the mayor of Salt Lake City and the Borough President of the Bronx are denying rumors that they are exploring the possibility of secession.' The Union is falling apart, Jack!"

"Gentlemen, please! Now is the time for a new plan. Only together will we triumph over diversity."

"Who's talking to them?"

"You mean Fredericks? Nobody. They'll only talk to the Secretary of State."

"Well then, I'll talk to them."

"The hell you will! We need to send them a message that we're not playing around anymore."

"I agree."

"The NSA is ready to put some guys from their cyber-assault division on it. They're confident they can break through their computer security . . . shut the bank down."

"Whatever. That all sounds good."

"I also think we need to get the CIA in on this. They have a plan that I think will work."

"What plan is that?"

"A plan that's worked in more than one African nation."

Prince finishes a song.

After a long silence, an old man declares, "I told you we should've gone with Shirley Caesar!"

The room explodes, with everyone yelling about their favorite singer. Prince stands uncomfortably on stage, not sure what to do.

A woman's voice can be heard yelling over the others, "WHAT ABOUT STEVIE?!! WHAT ABOUT STEVIE?!!"

February 25

"The most creative people in the world, and they came up with that?"

"Hey, it was mostly old people at the Nation Time meetings," says Kendrick. "You know how old black people feel about Jesus."

"Mental note," says Donna.
"This will be a problem."

"We are gathered here, not only to celebrate the opening of the First Bank, a bank which we believe, will bring us great prosperity in the years to come, but to celebrate our nationhood. The people have chosen a name, and from this day forth, let the Republic of . . . Blackland—"

"Blackland? Blackland?!"

"It was either that or Martin Luther Kingland. Stop complaining."

". . . be a beacon of freedom to the world. And to honor our nation, we shall have the first playing of our national anthem, sung by the First Baptists Missouri Avenue Choir."

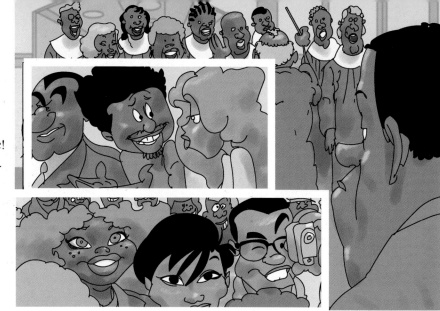

They sing to the tune of the *Good Times* theme:
"Blackland! Ain't it time we had a country?!
Blackland! Ain't it time for feelin' free?!
Blackland! Ain't it time for some justice!
Not gettin' hassled, not gettin' hustled...
Keepin' our heads over water,
makin' our way where we can.
It's our land so stay off! Blackland!!
Best believe we ain't soft! Blackland!!
Scratchin' and survivin'! Blackland!
Used to be Americans!! Blackla-aand!
Ain't we lucky we got it!
Blacklaaaaaaaaaand!"

"Well, god damn . . ."

WELL, GOD DAMN !!

"I heard that, Brother Jeff—" He notices
the garbage truck. "Well, god damn. . ."

"Listen, we're not waiting for a welfare check. We are the New African People's Party, and we've been trying for weeks to see—"

"The President is not taking any visits from revolutionary or radical organizations at this time."

Several Black Hebrew Israelites throw their hands up in frustration and walk out, complaining.

"But we were told yesterday that if we came back today—"

"I'm sorry, but I can't let you up."

"'TEN-HUT! GENERAL COMIN'!"

"Look! It's General Roscoe!"

"Yeah . . . So I know you new in town. I know all the fine women in this city. You that . . . outta town fine."

"Yes, um . . . General Roscoe, sir."

"So you need to get down with the General, let me show y'all around. Bring your friend, too. I know a guy who likes them bougie broads."

"You know, you giving your number out to every man with a gold tooth is slightly counter-revolutionary."

"Now, now … Didn't we come here to bond with the locals?"

"I can't believe they won't even let us see Fredericks."

"Hakeem, your cousin at MIT, the one that got arrested for hacking into all those porn sites."

"It wasn't porn sites …"

"Hakeem! Tony got arrested for hacking into porn sites?!"

"He wasn't hacking into porn sites!"

"Really? What kind of porn?"

"Like that matters? Ohmygod I'm so disappointed in—"

"Who cares? He's a hacker and can dig up Fred's address."

"Yeah, he got audited a few years back, so he hacked the IRS."

"And he got rid of the audit?"

"Naw, he found the Treasury Secretary's home address and waited for him to come home and punched him in the mouth. He's a really smart guy but a little …You know—"

"Were they black porn sites?"

69

"What's this?"

"New remote bulletproof security doors. Now that we got dough, it's nothing but the best. Fred, I'd like you to meet your new security team. I'd trust each of these men with my life."

"This is my cousin Earl, my Uncle James, and my other cousin Tony. Earl once saved my life by whuppin' the cowboy shit out of Bobby Cason in the fifth grade. Tony used to do security for the Gap Band."

"Thank you for your service, gentlemen."

"You shouldn't be standing so close to that window."

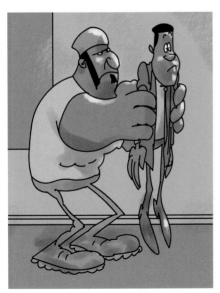

"And for . . . being pro-active."

"And this is Jim Kelly. Cinema star, martial arts icon, and all around Badazz Mofo."

"That was a long time ago. I mostly play tennis now . . ."

"So how you holding
up, Mr. President?"

"Like a martyr-
to-be . . ."

"I know it's hard,
but you have to
learn to relax.
We're winning."

"There are so many things . . .
I still think the Roscoe thing
was a mistake. You know he's
opened recruiting offices?"

"I told you, I'm not
scared of Roscoe."

"What are you
scared of?"

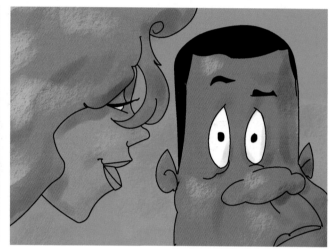

"Dimples."

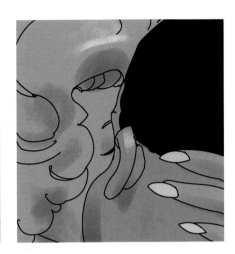

"But . . . what about John?"

"John's into overweight Asian women."

"Well I have to say it's great to have you here to clarify some of the things we've been hearing about Blackland. So, you're saying you guys are not communists?"

"Communists? Oh, no . . . Look, baby, we got Jesus on our flag, and He wasn't no communist."

"Well, that sure is Jesus and he sure wasn't a communist."

The television, music, and lights all shut off.

"Wow," says Donna, "you didn't have to clap or nothing ..."

"He's part of the history of this city! You 'shamed of yo' history?"

"Ashamed?! Just 'cause I don't want to see Ike Turner on the five dollar bill?!"

The lights go out.

March 1

"Any chance this is an accident?"

"No . . . but no need to worry, we have redundant generators and backup units for the bank."

"So what do we do?"

"We've pissed them off now, but it doesn't matter."

"Look, three hundred years ago, religion was the strongest force in the world. Then it was government. Now, it's commerce. Do you understand what we've done here? We've started a flow of money so massive it can't be stopped—and they know it."

"That's nice, John, but they've cut our power and it's still winter. What do we do about the people?"

"Tell 'em to buy blankets with all the extra welfare money I gave them. I don't really care . . ."

"That's not good enough."

"I hate to break it to you, Fred, but when you secede from a country bad things happen. There will be inconveniences. The people will just have to suck it up or leave—Now if you'll excuse me, I'm freezing my ass off—"

"Mr. Roberts . . ."

"Is there a problem?"

"Yes sir. Someone's trying to hack into the mainframe. Someone who knows what he's doing."

"Who?"

"Untraceable. My guess is it's government."

"Can you keep them out?"

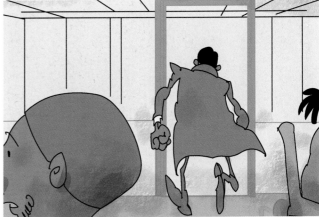

"Not for long. We may need to take the bank offline."

"We don't want to do that unless we absolutely have to. Hold 'em as long as you can. I'll think of something."

"Dammit . . . I can't see anything!"

"Need a light, Mr. President?"   "Ambush!"

"Huh?! No wait—"

"Stop! Ohmygod! Stop beating up my people!"   "Grab the President!!"

"I can't see him!"   "KIAI!"   "OOF!"
"You broke my glasses!"

"Wait! Everyone just wait! WAIT!"

"I'm such a bad leader." "So you found out where the President lives using a . . . computer?" "Yes, Lurch. Welcome to the 21st century." "Why are you here?" "I have—" "I have the solution to your energy problem. Did I mention it's an honor to meet you?"

"I know this is an odd place to meet, but . . . it's much safer than City Hall, believe me. You guys realize they've got that whole building bugged by now." "To be honest, I don't know how you've survived this long. You know they got satellites now that get you from space. One day you're walking down the street and—ZAP! This is wonderful pie . . . Really, really good. I taste boysenberries." "Um, not to rush you, but . . ."

"Huh? Oh, right . . . So after I left MIT I decided I would spend the rest of my career solving humankind's energy problems . . . You know, get us off fossil fuels, save the environment, etc." "And you succeeded?" "That's the thing . . . I was about 25 years too late! A bunch of guys, I'm talking since the early seventies . . . already been there and done that. I mean . . . people don't realize—"

"Look, it's the biggest conspiracy in the world. I'm talking solar fusion hybrid engines whose only waste is pure water. Two-dollar fuel cells that can power office buildings for half a year. Heck, you could run this whole city off algae if you wanted. It's all old news—but they don't want anyone to know about it."

"Who is 'they'?"

"You name it. OPEC, Standard Oil, heck, even the Detroit auto manufacturers have freelance assassins that hunt Merlins."

"A 'Merlin' is a code name for someone like Sam here who creates alternative energy devices."

"Right. 'Cause the world's economy is based on oil. If suddenly nobody needs oil . . ."

"Okay, so you say you can get us our power back . . .what'll it take?"

"Well, it'll take a few days for the city. More if you want to convert the cars."

"Fine."

"And I'll need security. Twenty-four hours."

"The N.A.P.P.'s can do that!"

"Okay, okay, fine . . . How much will it cost?"

"The whole city? About sixty bucks."

"Can I have some more pie?"

"Waitress!"

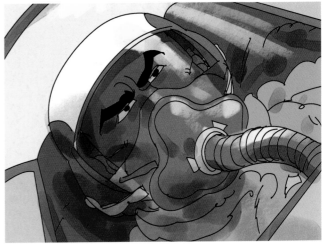

"Headhunter 1-2, this is Headhunter 1-1, I am engaged defensive!"

"Call for help all you want, boy, your ass is mine."

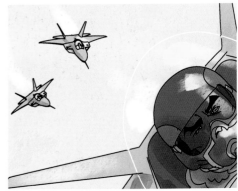

"You ain't gettin' away, boy! We goin' ship what's left of you back to that East St. Louis garbage heap in a box, you hear me, Washington?"

"Oh ... I'm gettin' away, all right ..."

"Damn this boy's slippery."

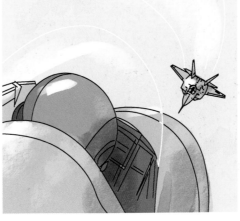

"Smoke, he got up over me, you got 'em?"

"I lost him, sir!"

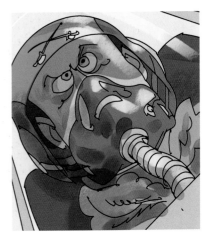

"Shit! Where is he?!"

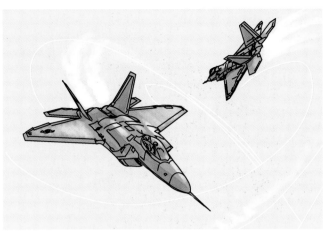

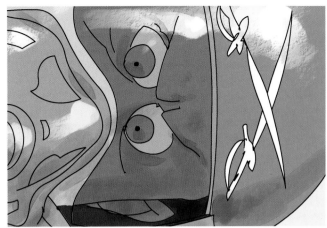

"This is Cowboy 1-2, I got no joy on Washington . . . he's nowhere in sight and I got negative radar contacts."

"Captain Washington, report your status. Answer me, Captain, that's an order."

"Mr. President, I—"

"Call me Fred."

"Okay . . . Fred . . . look, I'll get right to the point. You need me as your advisor."

"Is that so?"

"Yes. I know you have to be careful who you trust—"

"Exactly. So why don't we wait and see—"

"Because there's no time to wait. You need my help now; I don't know much about the people you're in this with, but they're not telling you what you need to be told."

"And what do I need to be told?"

"That this isn't a business venture, Fred, it's a revolution. If you don't start treating it like one right now, you're as good as dead."

"They can't stop us. We've started a flow of money so massive they'll have to make a deal. Commerce runs the world now, not governments."

"And who told you that bedtime story? John Roberts?"

"Fred, they only reason they haven't killed you yet is because you're too popular. But even popularity couldn't save the Kennedys."

"Fred, you're the most dangerous man in the world. You won't see them coming until it's too—"

There's a loud roar from overhead.

"What the . . . ? !"

"A military jet . . ."

"You're hired."

Fred's phone rings. He answers.

"Mr. Mayor President, sir. I think you need to see this . . ."

"Boogie?!"

"Boogie! What have . . . Why?!"   "Heard you guys could use an Air Force!"   "We are in soooooo much trouble . . ."

"Would someone like to explain?"   "Ma'am, Capt. George Washington, but you can call me Boogie Down, declaring my intention to defect."

"I was born and raised in East St. Louis, ma'am. This is my home."

"But, George . . . they'll hang you for this!"   "They'll hang you first."

"Sam? It's Fred. You got ten minutes, then we're calling it a night."

"We're almost there, Mr. President."

"What's wrong with you?"

"I'm wondering how we're going to get out of this alive. Kabilah was saying—"

"Yeah—what's up with her? You smash them bougie cheeks yet?"

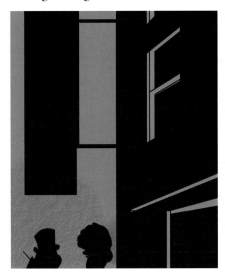

"Well, I'll be damned . . ."

"The wiring was so old it actually made the job more complicated. But now that's done, we can go building by building and be done in a few—"

"I told you I wouldn't let you down!"

"Um-hmm . . . 'President Pa-dussy.'"

"The results of yesterday's vote are as follows. The face on the twenty-five-cent piece will be Fred Fredericks, and the face on the dime piece will be Sade. And now the floor will continue to hear debates on our two candidates for the Blackland nickel—Tupac Shakur and Biggie Smalls."

"But what about the flow? Biggie's flow killed 'Pac's!!"

"All I'm sayin'—is let me talk! Let me talk!! Tupac lyrics, if you listen—"

"Tupac was a bitch!"

"What?! Say that again! Say that shit again!"

"I said, Tupac was a BITCH!"

BANG! BANG!
WOOOWOOOWOOOWOOO

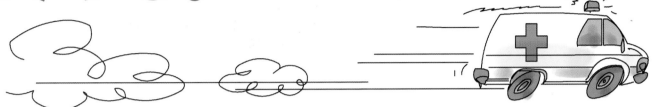

"Every time we block them they come at us a different way."

"It's gotta be NSA. We have to take the bank offline or they'll wipe us out."

"We take the bank offline and we all go home."

"Why wasn't I told about this earlier?"

"The bank is my concern."

"The bank is the country's concern!"

"Guys!"

"I know a hacker. That's how we found Fred. I know a guy who could help!"

"Of course you do."

"George . . ." She pauses dramatically. ". . . Are you a defector?"

"Last I checked, the U.S. Government had not recognized East St. Louis as a separate nation. You can't defect to your own country . . .

"I'm sorry . . . I—"

"This VTOL F-22 Raptor is a relatively short-range fighter, but fully fueled it could strike targets in any midwestern city, and could reach as far as Washington, D.C. ..."

"And even our radar systems can't track it?"

"With a skilled pilot it would be nearly impossible. Captain Washington was one of the best in the Corps."

"Guys, maybe we could just ask for it back?"

"Ask for it back? They just stole a fully armed eighty million dollar aircraft—"

"They didn't steal it, the pilot defected—"

"... that could destroy the White House —or Air Force One—before anyone knows it's even there, and you think they're going to just give it back!"

"Yes! If you would just let me talk to them, yes!"

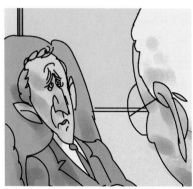
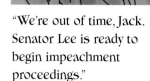

"Jack, we've set the invasion two weeks from today."

"What?!"

"We're out of time, Jack. Senator Lee is ready to begin impeachment proceedings."

"Senator Lee is Commander in Chief now? When was he elected President?"

"Actually, if you think about it, neither one of us was elected President!"

"Get it . . . 'cause I really didn't win the election. Remember, this is how this whole thing started . . ."

"What about the CIA plan?"

"They have two weeks."

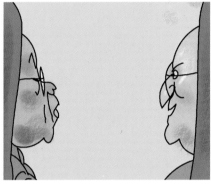

"What is the CIA plan?"

"That's need-to-know information."

"You realize they have more public support than this administration. Has anyone seen this?"

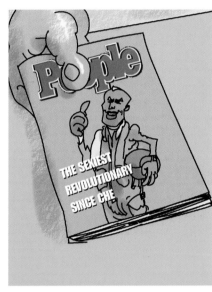

"That was before he had a loaded gun pointed at the head of everyone in the continental United States. We spin this right he'll be as popular as Yasser Arafat pissing on the Torah at a bar mitzvah."

"Okay, Richard. That was disgusting."

"Done."   "That's it?!"

"We're secure! I've never seen anything like this ... how—"

"A year ago I broke into the NSA computers to see if all that X-Files shit was real ... picked up all the tricks of their cyber assault division."

"So was the X-Files stuff real?"

"Are you kidding? They got this satellite that can shoot a nigga from space. Crazy. That'll be ten million dollars, Mr. Roberts."

"Ten million!"

"You can give me ten now, or I'll take thirty later."

"Now that Fred Fredericks has a loaded gun pointed at the head of every American, we're seeing the support for Fredericks decline drastically. Look at these recent poll numbers. Support for the East St. Louis rebellion has dropped 10 points in one week to—"

"Not getting hassled . . . Not getting hustled . . ."

"Good morning, Omar. Still in town?"

"I'm afraid so. . . I have another mission, brother. Very serious."

March 10

"There's half. You get the other half on completion, as usual."

"What's the gig?"

"That guy on the news in East St. Louis."

"Fredericks? Why would the auto makers want to off Fredericks?"

"He found a Merlin—"

"Assassinate Fredericks?"

"He is dabbling in energy technologies that threaten the entire Arab world. Have you ever heard the term Merlin?"

"He had no choice! They cut the power to the city!"

"You have your orders, my friend. Islam calls for your service."

89

"What does this has to do with Islam?"

"It kind of has to do with Islam indirectly, I mean . . . if you think about it—"

"You actually want me to be an Arab terrorist in this day and age? That's so . . . stereotypical."

"Spare me the righteous indignation, Habib! You own a 7-11"

"So?"

"So it's not like you're an ice skater or a fireman! I mean, you're not exactly breaking down barriers with this convenience store. Know what you are to these people? You're Apu. What, you think we don't get *The Simpsons* in Saudi Arabia? We get it. Satellite dishes. You're nothing more than Apu!"

"Apu's Indian—"

"Same shit! You've been a sleeper for so long, my friend. You've forgotten your loyalties . . . and you know what we do to traitors."

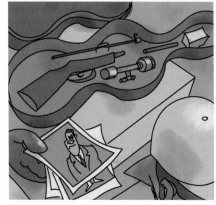

"Here is your primary target. President Fred Fredericks—"

"I don't need surveillance photos, the man comes in here every day!"

"Morning Habib!"

"This has been the scene in dozens of cities since President Caldwell's statement that he is preparing a military invasion of Blackland moved the nation closer to a second civil war. Twenty-four people were injured in Washington this morning during unrest—"

The phone rings.

"Fredericks."

The voice on the phone growls, "Fred . . . you's a dead red NIGGA!!"

"Haaaah! I got you, cuz!"

"It's a chess game now. The only way we survive is with leverage. We need an ally. Somebody that can hurt the United States who we can get to intervene on our behalf."

"That's if you want to win. If you only want to survive, just sell the rest of us down the river—"

They both laugh.

"That's what your partners will probably do, anyway."

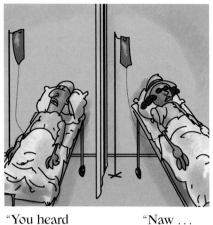

"You heard who got the nickel?" "Naw . . . Who?"

"Bitch-ass Will Smith." "Damn. F'real? That punk-ass?"

"So where to after this?" "I think the elementary school, then lunch with President Fredericks."

"Well, we're just so glad you came to visit us here." "Well, it's not every day you get your face on a nickel."

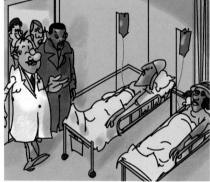

"Guys, I have a surprise for you!" "Hey, fellas, how y'all feelin'?" "Will Smith?!" "Damn, dawg? What you doing here?"

"Well, I don't know if you heard, but I got the nickel—" "Yeah, we heard about that, dawg. Congrats!" "I'm a big fan of your music, man."

"Your movies, too, dawg. Them shits is tight." "Well thank you both. I hear y'all will be up and outta here in no time. Take it easy."

"You know . . . he really is a nice guy." "But that don't mean you gotta ride his dick like that."

92

"That's it, nigga—I'm sick of your—"

"The reality is there's too much money at stake. All of the President's top corporate contributors have millions invested in that bank of yours. If he shuts you down—he won't have a reelection campaign. That's what Fred and Roberts don't get."

"So if he doesn't want to shut us down, what does he want?"

"He wants somebody in charge here who . . . knows how to share."

"Oh . . . so y'all just trying to shake niggas down . . ."

"Do you have any idea how much they're making off that bank?"

The agent tells him how much.

"Now . . . how much of that are they giving you?"

"You guys are making that much money!"

"Yeah . . ."

"Fred!! What are you doing with it?!"

"Obviously not spending it on decorating-"

"Well . . . it's complicated."

"Fred . . . do you realize what you can do with all that money? You could start over completely . . . build the perfect society—"

"Yes, but..."

"No. I don't think you understand. Fred, with that kinda money you could put a computer on every desk. Pay schoolteachers like ... basketball players! I'm talking a complete environmental cleanup. Shut down the smokestacks. Deleaden the soil. Rebuild.

"You pay a ridiculous premium to attract the world's best researchers and doctors. You build the hospitals, a research university ...

"You legalize drugs, which will get rid of the gangs ... Fred, this won't just be good for East St. Louis. The world will see what you've done and demand it where they live! This, Fred—this is the revolution. It doesn't matter how much money you make. It's what you do with it that will permanently, irrevocably, and most definitely bring the white supremacist power structure to its cowardly, diabolical knees!"

"God I'm such a nerd."

"It's time for a budget meeting."

"Fred, I've never asked this of another human being, because I don't believe in making fun of the afflicted—but are you retarded?"

"I mean, do you occasionally choke on your own spit? 'Cause that's a sign of retardation."

"You're out of line."

"This budget is out of line! A ten-million-dollar environmental cleanup? Five million to education? How many kids live in this city?!"

"What I'm asking for is a drop in the bucket compared to—"

"Fifty million in 'wealth redistribution' is one hell of a drop, Fred!"

"I think this is Fred's term paper on the joys of Socialism. Did you get a good grade, Fred?"

"Yo, f'real . . . there ain't gonna be too many more jokes on the President."

"You got that right."

"I can't even take this seriously."

"Uh-huh . . . I heard there was a budget meeting going on. Looks like President Fred still has a problem using the phone. I want to talk about the military budget."

"Military budget?"

"I want 300 million."

"Hold on . . . did mental retardation just mutate into an airborne virus?"

"Watch your tone with the General."

"Well, I won't watch mine. If you want to talk about funding, you request a meeting with me. But since you're here . . . what the hell do you need 300 million dollars for, Roscoe? What are going to win, a ground campaign? Invade Chicago?"

"Nala!?"

"Whoa, everybody calm down!"

"Our agreement stands. You take orders from me. Now remove yourself from this room before I have you shot."

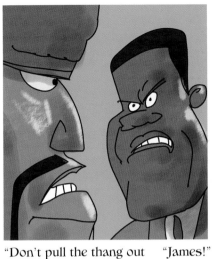

"Don't pull the thang out
unless you fittin' to bang."   "James!"

cli-CLACK

"Our mission here
is accomplished."

"This is my
country."

"Fred!"

"This
ain't the
time,
Donna."   "Dammit, Fred! If you
wanted to play Romper
Room with Miss . . . Lola
Granola in there you just
should have told me!"

"Donna,
look at me.
Look at
me!"

"Do I look like I'm in
the mood for a god-
damn soap opera? Don't
you think I have enough
to worry about?"   "Then you
shouldn't
be worried
about some
little bitch!"

"Unless
that bitch is
you, right?"

"You were supposed to be the
tough one. Donna—get your
priorities straight. We need you."

"Yeah, gurl
. . . that's my
nigga right—"

"I just think you
should calm down—"

"Ain't shit gonna be calm. Oh no,
these niggas done lost their minds."

"Yeah, it's me. I'm down."

"Roscoe . . . what are you going to do?"

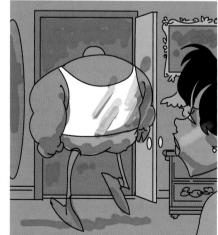

"You'll definitely go down in the history books for this one. But you're not like these other guys . . . you've got something to lose."

"I had something to lose. Now I got everything to gain."

"We can unfreeze your accounts."

"Where'd you go to school, boy? They pick you up at Yale? Cornell?"

"Well, at Cornell, they should have taught you that the one billion dollars you took from me ain't shit compared to the 10 billion I'll control in the next four years. So if the government thinks I'm gonna run away from being the richest man in the world because some Ivy League spook prick who can't do simple math says 'Boo' they got another think coming. So why don't you run along and fax me a list of who I need to pay off to keep you guys off my back. Now unless you plan on making a deposit, the door is thataway."

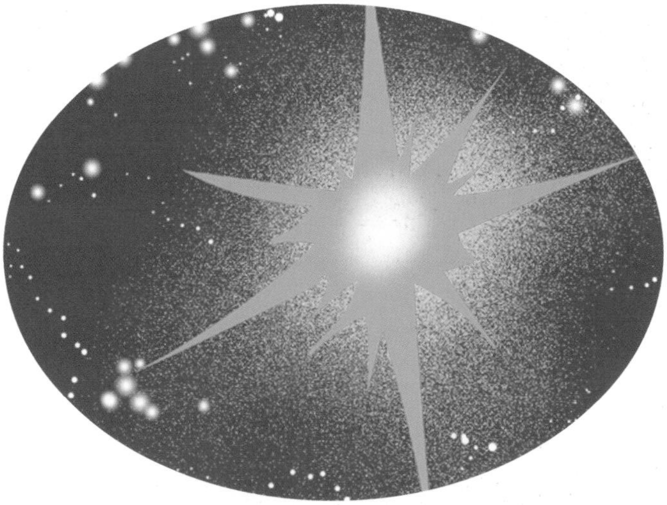

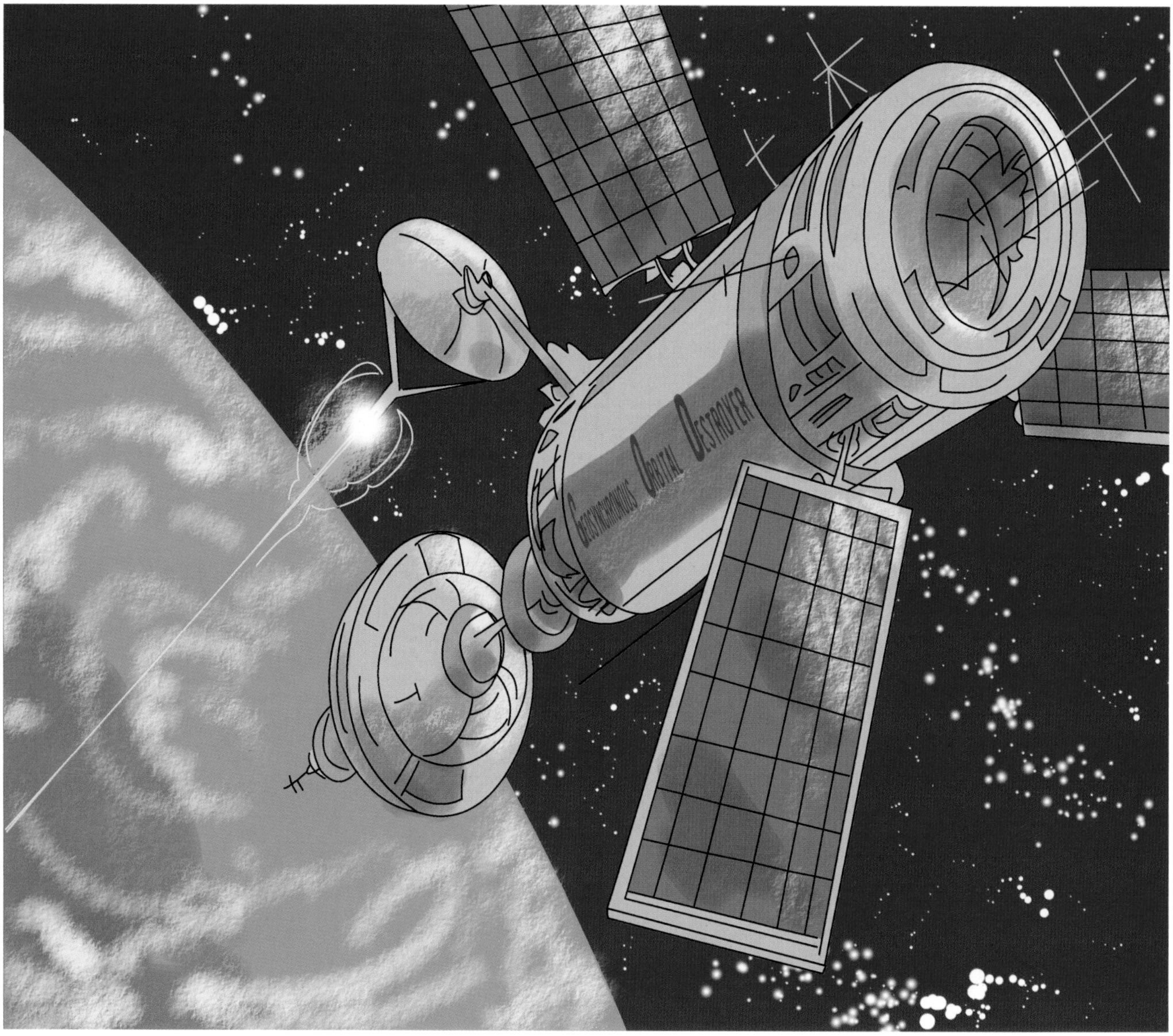
Geosynchronous Orbital Destroyer

From down the street, the soft whine of Sam McFadden's fusion-powered scooter can be heard.

"Told you."

"...at the U.S.-Blackland border, where Marine and Army units are starting to assemble. In everybody's mind the same question—will it really come to this..."

"I just can't believe... Nala..."

Roberts and Donna arrive at the door. Fred pushes the button on his keychain to let them in.

"What happened to you?"

"They tried to kill him last night."

"It's over, Fred—"

"Says who?"

"They tried to kill me!"

"Really? Well, when you secede from a country bad things happen. There will be inconveniences."

"We can still make a deal—"

"I'm sure some of us already have—"

"Fred, I'm trying to save us all—"

"Everybody out. Now."

"Everybody."

"Whoever you are, I just hope I'm there when he finds out what you're really up to."

"If you're smart enough, you will be."

"We call it quits before they come in shooting. We spare them the embarrassment of a massacre and they spare our lives, is that it?"

"That's it."

"Fred we had our fun! We changed the world, you got payback on Caldwell! We won and can still walk away with our lives and enough money—"

"No."

"Fred, I know you believe in all this 'we shall overcome' shit, but we can't beat them!"

"All that we've done . . .why do you hold on to what can't be done?"

"I've put more wealth and power in your lap than you could have ever dreamed! Hell, you can be the next President! I give you Donna, and you're gonna wreck that over some eggheaded bitch? What is it about failure that you find so appealing, Fred?"

"What . . . oh I get it . . . you want to save the niggas. Well let me tell you— you can't save niggas in a year, you can't save 'em in 50 years, and you definitely can't save 'em if you're dead!"

"I'm taking the money Fred."

"You no longer control the bank, John. I had Kabilah's hacker give me a back door."

"No . . . that's impossible."

"I told you I wasn't gonna let you use these people to make a buck."

"You son of a bitch."

"I'll let you take 50 million. Leave now and you've got a 48-hour head start before the shooting begins. You can disappear, John. Start over. Take it or leave it."

"If you're lucky enough to live through this . . . you'll have to live with the deaths of hundreds, maybe thousands of people. Is it worth it, Fred?"

"John is taking some cash and cutting his losses. You are welcome to join him, Donna."

"Fred, this was never about—"

"Yes or no, Donna."

"If you have a plan I'll stay. I want to win."

"Good. I do have an idea, Donna, but I need you on a plane tonight."

"Okay."

"Fred, John had a point— The people. We can't just arbitrarily put all of their lives in danger like this."

"No, we can't."

"Give it to us straight . . . what's the worst that can happen?"

"I don't know. People will die. Maybe . . . lots of people."

The crowd murmurs.

"And if we surrender?"

"Me, Donna, Boogie . . . we'll be executed for treason."

The crowd mumbles its displeasure.

"For you guys, things will just go back to the way they were before."

"Does that mean no money?"

"The money will be gone."

The crowd roars loudly in disapproval.

"I lost my arm serving in the Marines during the invasion of Panama City. It was a city full of black people, and the Marines came in. And what happened was black bodies got pushed into mass graves. It can happen here."

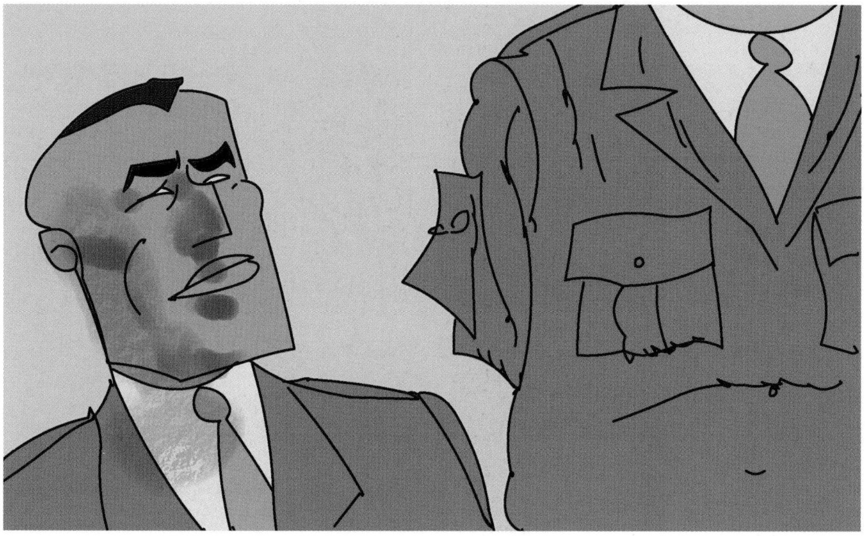

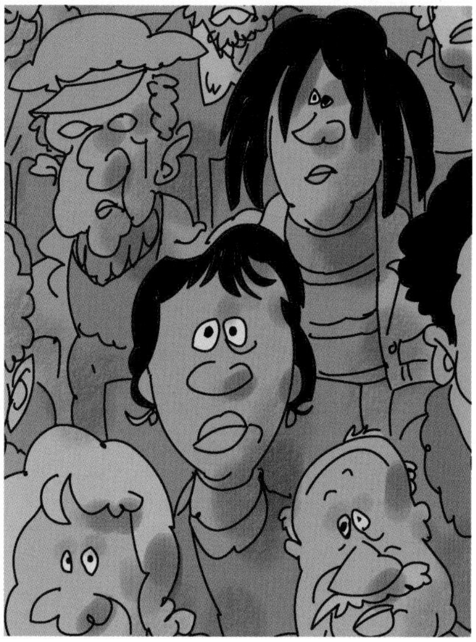

"But even with all that I've been through . . . I'm proud that my son is a soldier ready to fight for what he believes. Nations are baptized with the blood of patriots. That's how it is."

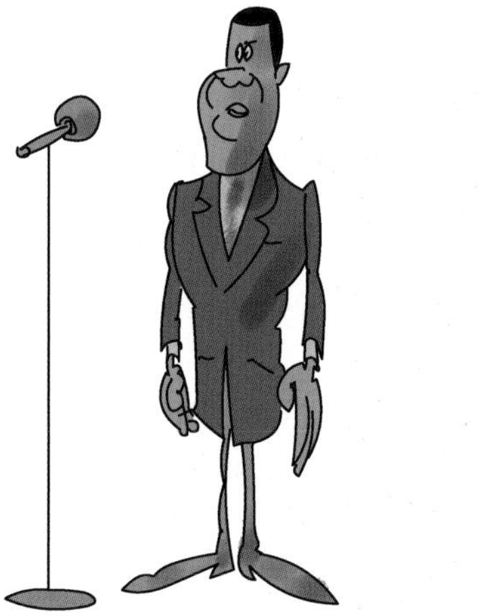

"We'll have the vote now. Those who believe that we should protect our borders with force . . . stand now."

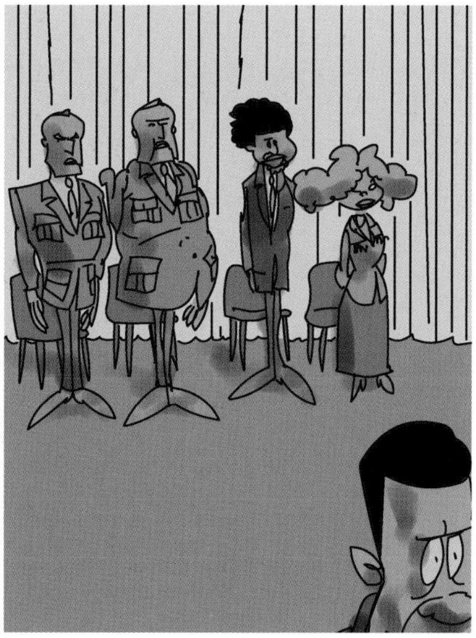

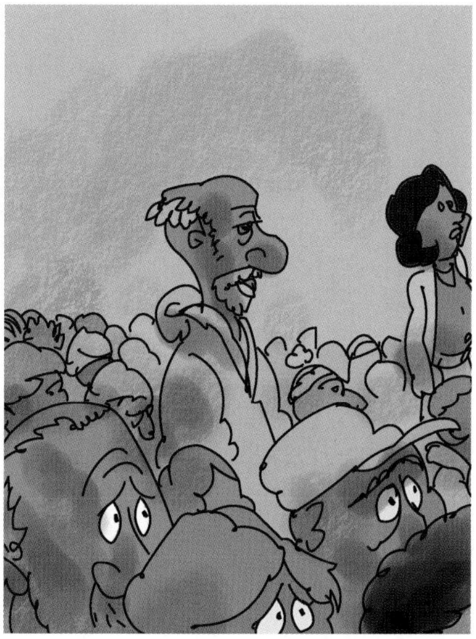

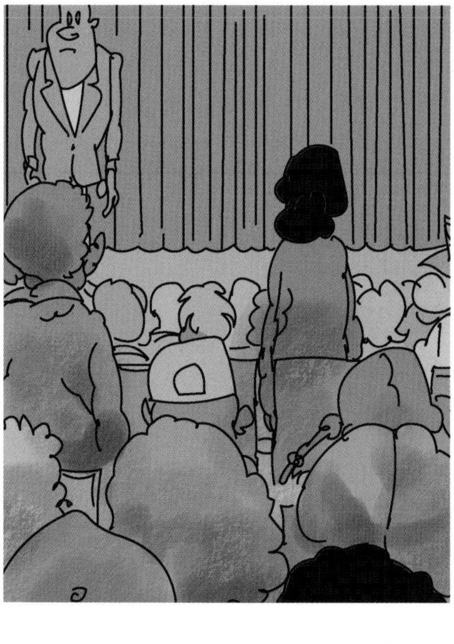

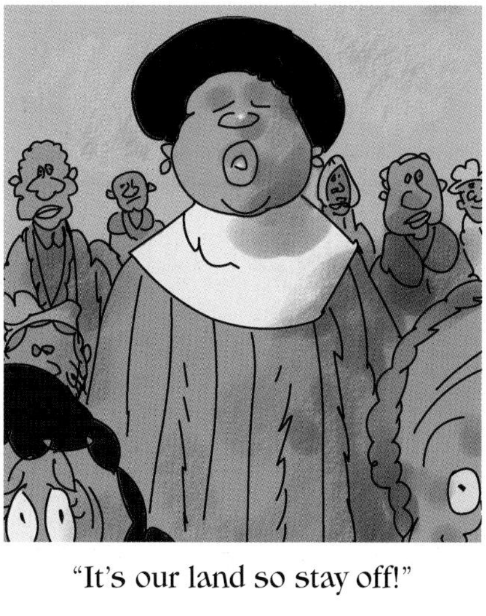

"It's our land so stay off!"

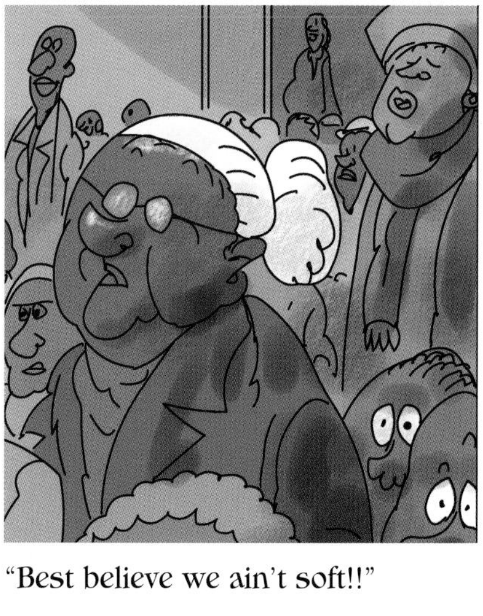

"Best believe we ain't soft!!"

"Scratchin' and survivin'!!"

"Used to be Americans!"

"Ain't we lucky we got it . . ."

"Blacklaaaaaaaand!"

MARCH 15

"The enemy looks like you, talks like you, could be your own brother. But we took an oath to defend this nation against all enemies foreign and domestic, and that is what we will do. Marines."

"Kabilah. If I die today—"

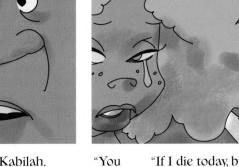

"You won't die today."

"If I die today, but through some miracle . . . this country survives, we owe it all to you."

"You won't die today. I'm going to protect you."

"Thank you for coming here, Kabilah. Thank you for wanting to help."

"My name is . . . Shannon Randall."

"Cowboy 1-l, this is Home Plate, you are weapons free on the rogue Raptor. I repeat, you are clear to engage Captain Washington on sight."

"Roger that, Home Plate. If he comes off the dirt we'll get 'em."

SAUDI ARABIA

"East St. Louis Air Control, this is the Marine Three. We are entering your airspace."

The radio crackles, "We got you, Marine Three. Welcome to Blackland."

"Kendrick Wallace. I'm the Foreign Minister of the Republic of Blackland. Let's do this."

"You can't be serious."

"Before we were the Army that ran this city, we were the crew that ran these streets. Ain't nuthin' changed."

"He's there. Got up early and went into the office. Kabilah's there too, plus his security."

"How many?"

"I saw three."

"We fixin' to move out in five."

"Roscoe . . . you don't have to do this."

"Whose side are you on, huh?"

"Yours, honey . . . it's just . . . you can't trust the CIA. I'd hate for something to happen to you."

"You let me worry about that."

"What's going on?"

"Get in the van, Fred. Now."

"Enough of this! I would like to speak to Fred Fredericks!"

"The President is indisposed."

"Young man, whoever you are, I don't think you understand the magnitude of this situation. Do you realize that the Marines are crossing the border in three hours?"

"No they ain't."

"And why not?"

"Because you'll be facing the largest energy crisis in history."

"We'll be facing what?!"

A phone on the conference table rings.

"This is the Foreign Minister . . . Ah yes, we were awaiting your call . . . the Secretary is right here."

"This is the Secretary of . . . Secretary General Akbar, what a surprise."

"Well I don't understand why OPEC would be concerned with—"

"Yes. I know what a Merlin is . . ."

"Yes . . . yes, within the hour."

"Get me the President. Now."

"What's going on?"

"We couldn't risk telling you earlier, I'm sorry."

"Look."

"Jesus . . . who are they?"

There is a knock on the van door.

"Fred, can Boogie get in the air?"

"Boogie, this is Fred. Stand by, I may need you over at City Hall."

"Standing by, Mr. President."

"Fred. You there? It's Roscoe, man. I need to holla at you, bruh."

"Open the door, Fred."

Fred presses the button on his keychain.

"It's a setup! That bitch set us up! Get out of the building now!"

"Shut the door, Fred!"

"Shit!"

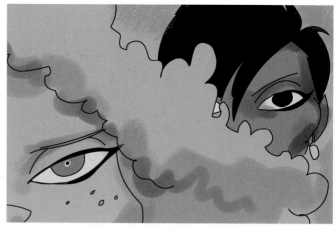

"That glass won't hold them forever."

"I—I can't . . ."

"It's not enough to be ready to die, Fred. You have to be ready to kill."

"Once he escapes from that building, we're all dead. One day he will come back for all of us."

"Boogie, destroy City Hall."

"Our City Hall?"

"Yes!"

"Black Angel 1, I have Mavericks locked on . . ."

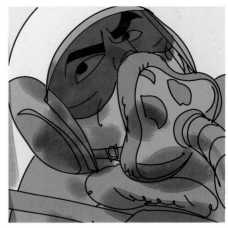

"Wait a minute, sir ... Someone's got radar lock on me!"

"Home Plate, this is Cowboy 1-2, we are engaged offensive with rogue Raptor, our position is—damn! Missed!"

"He's still locked! Fox-2 again!"

"Oh my god . . . it's two on one against Boogie!"

"Dammit, Smoke, he's gonna have your six, move it!"

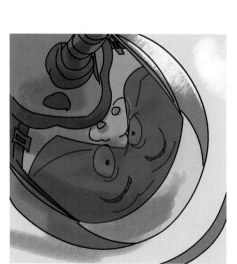

"Hurry,
Custer! Fox-2!
Shoot him!"

"I'm out of missiles!
Closing to guns range,
you gotta shake 'em—"

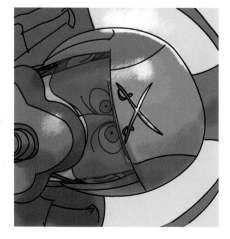

"Black Angel 1 to Fredericks, requesting permission to fire on enemy aircraft!"

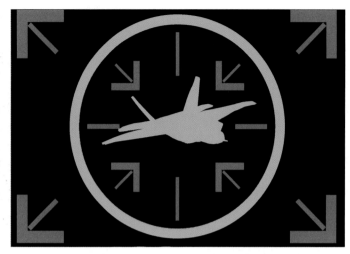

"What?!" asks Fred.   "I can't shoot until you say so!"

"Shoot, fool, shoot!"   "Roger. Black Angel 1, Fox-2!"

"Sure hope that
wasn't one of ours."

"We can't risk using a Blackhawk while that
F-22 is up there . . . Yes sir. Force Recon will
go in on foot to the crash site."

"They're moving in! Can anyone hear me? They're coming!"

If you would like to make a call please hang up and try again.

"The Americans are coming! The Americans are coming!"

"They're coming!"

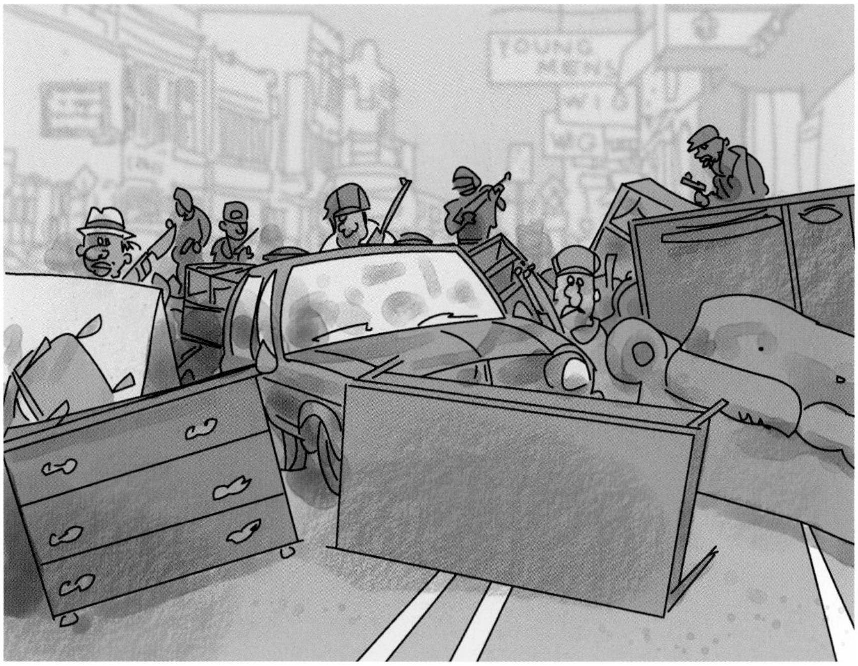
YOUNG MENS
WIG

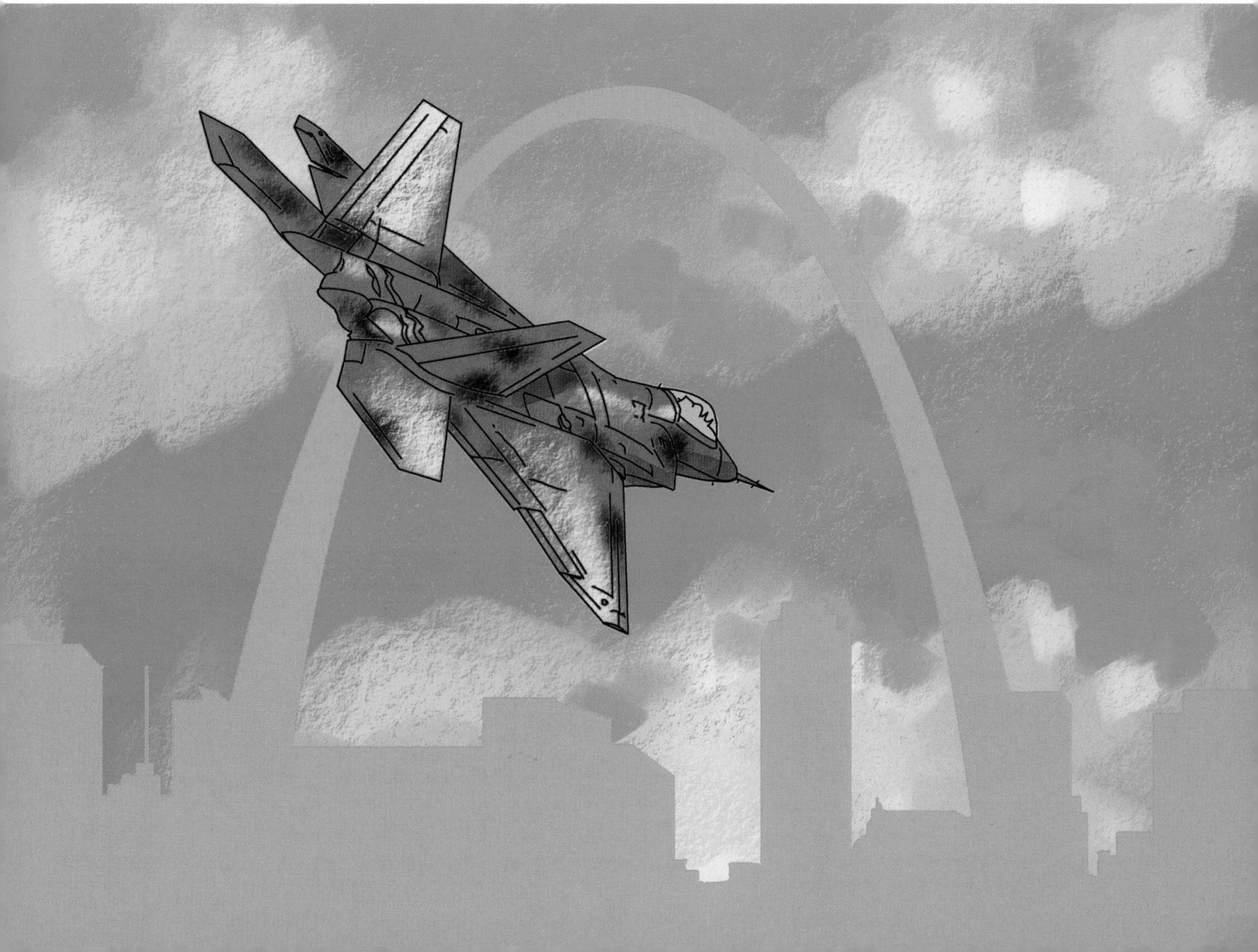

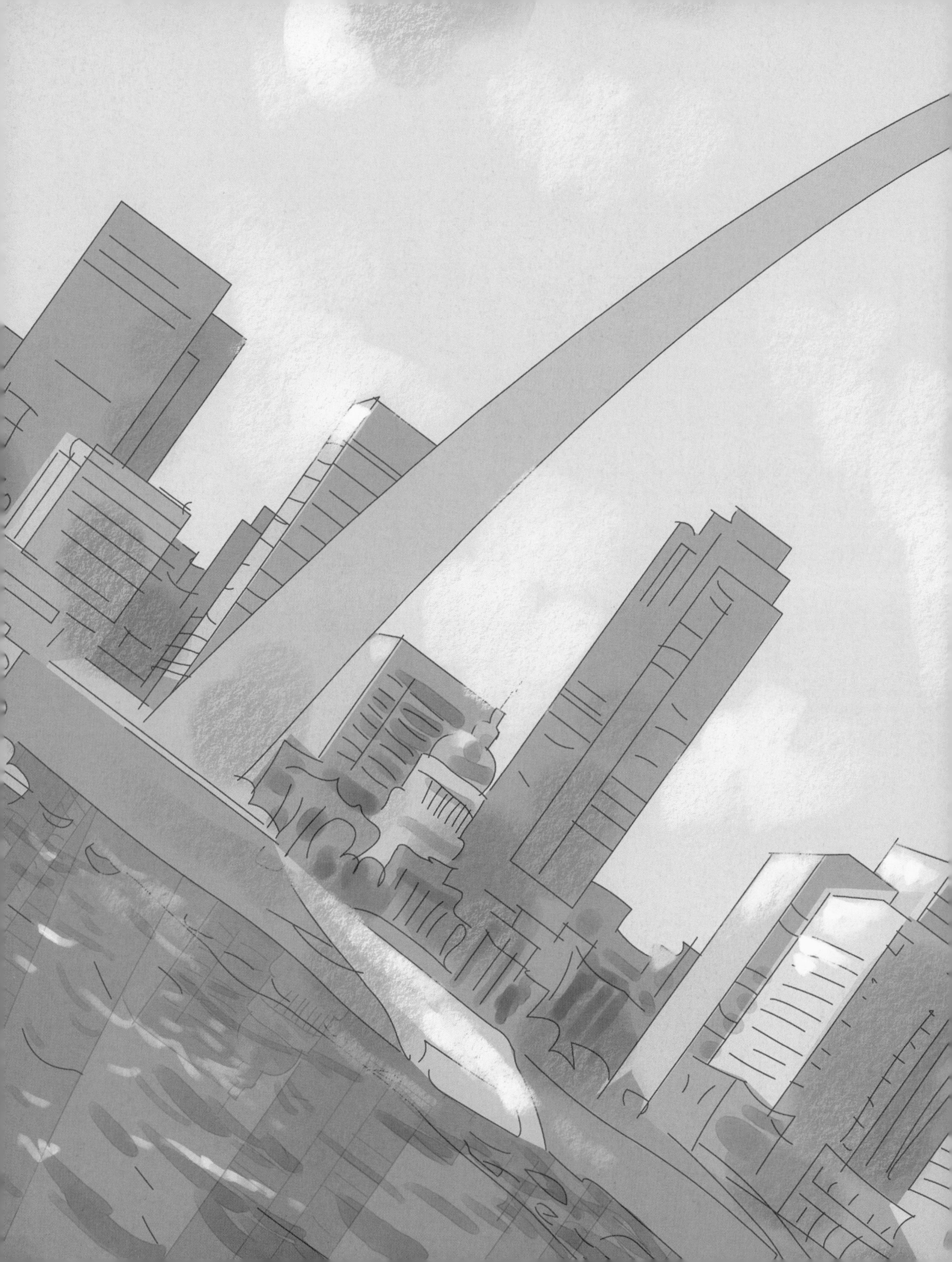

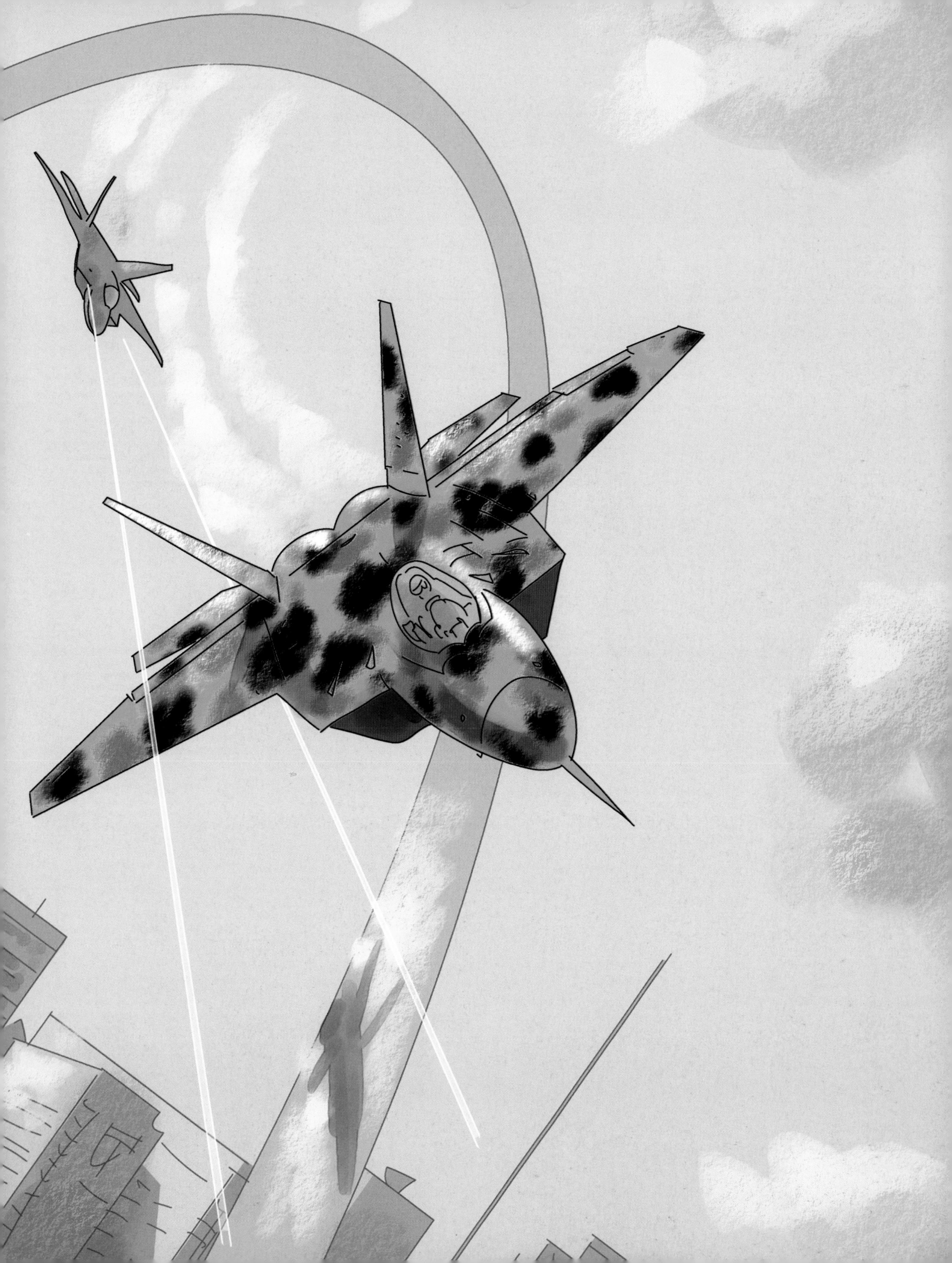

"That ain't
stoppin' no bullet."

"Them bullets'll go
through cars."

"Where   "There   "Everyone, hold
you   they   your fire till they
goin'?"   are!"   get closer!"

"I got two dozen. A few shooters
on the roof. Piece of cake."

"Jesus . . .   "This is the quickest
this isn't   way to the crash
right."   site, sir . . ."

"RPG. On my
mark."

"Mr. President . . . Fredericks has made some kind of deal with the Arabs . . . Yes, sir, I talked to Secretary General Akbar myself."

"They're threatening a complete oil embargo if we invade."

"Sir, under these circumstances we have to withdraw the troops until we know more."

"Sir?"   "Hold on . . ."

"Sir, we have a job to do—"   "Hold on! Just . . . let me think . . . Fire on my mark. Ready . . ."

A voice on the radio yells, "Abort! Abort! Recon squad, abort rescue, withdraw immediately—"

"They're running away!
Bitch niggas!"

"I'm on the leader . . ."

"What
are you
doing?"

"If Boogie can't destroy the
building in time we'll have to hit
'em as soon as they come out."

"Are you crazy?
The Marines are
on their way!"

"No! We won't
get another
chance!"

"C'mon!"

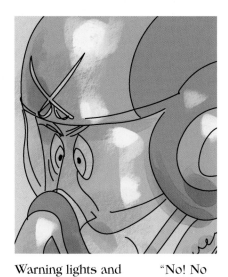  

Warning lights and alarms are flashing

"No! No ... you ..."

"C'mon, you know you wanna say it..."

"Nigger!"

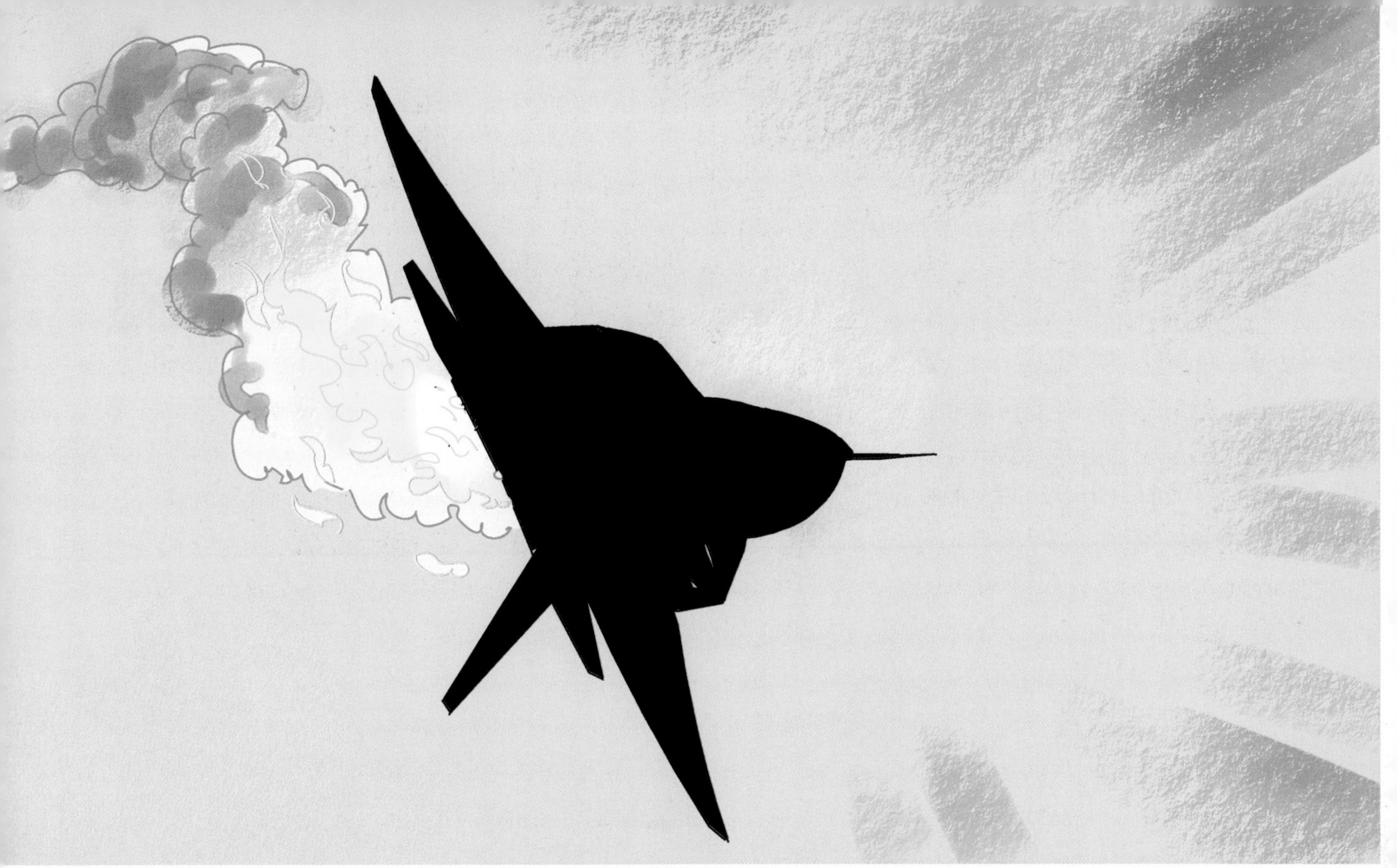

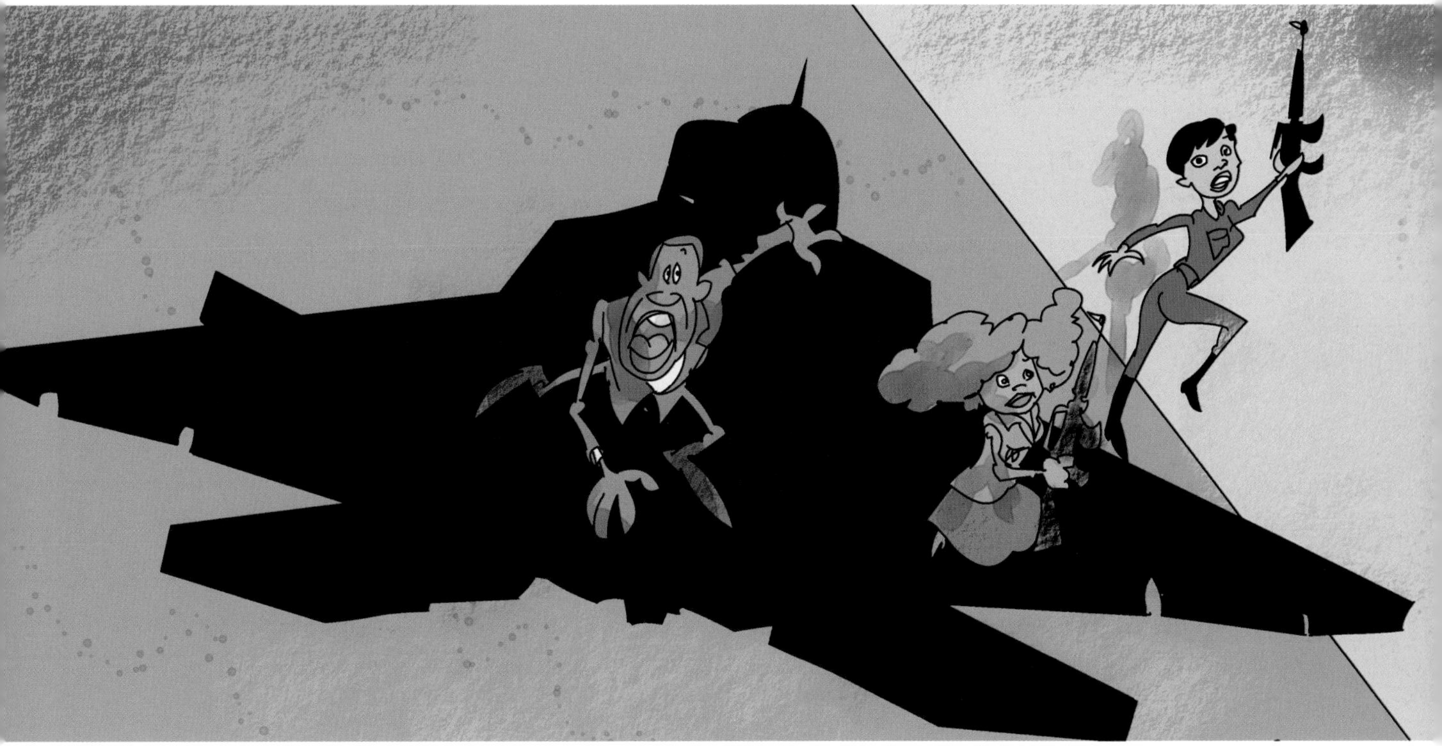

"Run!"

"So much for that   "Sir, you alright
moral dilemma."   down there?"

"We're all clear down   "Would you have really   "He was
here! Great shot, Boogie!"   shot your own boyfriend?"   selfish in bed."

"Yes, President Caldwell, I'm glad you see it that way. Excellent."

"He has agreed!"

"The President has called off the invasion. And I have your word—the world will never know of your 'alternative' energy sources."

"We will not use them, we will not export them. Ever again."

"And this ... Merlin ... Sam McFadden you will turn him over to us so we can kill him?"

"Now, Mr. Akbar ..."

"I had to try!"

You've reached Habib. Leave a message and I'll holla back. Peace.

"Dammit!" He starts dialing again.

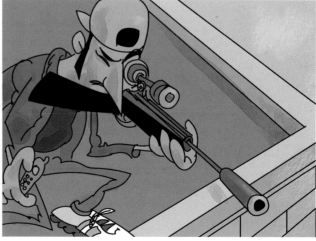

Habib's phone rings. He presses a button to stop the ring.

"The President has decided to continue to pursue diplomatic avenues to resolve this matter."

The reporters scream out questions about the dogfight.

"I can't comment on any of that."

"All that matters is we have, for the time being, averted war."

Habib's phone rings again.

"Could you make a decision, knowing it was the right thing to do, even if it might get you killed?"

"I can only hope that I would."

Shots ring out.

"He's all right!"

"Oh my GOD, IT HURTS!!"

"Oh, stop being a lil' punk-ass, sissy-ass bitch! You're alive!!"

"Look! He shot the sniper!"

"Habib?!"

"HAB-IZIB!!"   "PRESIDENT BIG DAWG!!"

"And so what started as a battle of political wills has ended in this, the signing of the U.S.–Blackland Treaty . . ."

SEPTEMBER 4

"You rub me up the wrong tree."

"You know, I may need a job in a couple years."

The choir sings,
"Just lookin' outta the window,
Watchin' the green grass grow.
Thinkin' how it all looks better now!"

"...It's our land so stay off!
Blackland!"

"...Scratchin' and survivin'! Blackland!
Used to be Americans!! Blacklaaaand!!"

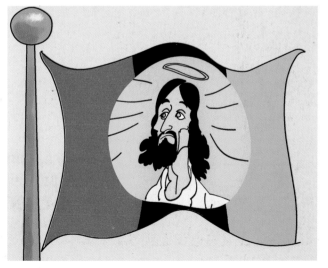

"Ain't we lucky we got it!"

"Blacklaaaa-aaaaaa-aaaaaaaand!"

THE END.

The first big book of Aaron McGruder's *The Boondocks,* more than four years and 800 strips of one of the most influential, controversial, and scathingly funny comics ever to run in a daily newspaper.

A Right to Be Hostile

1-4000-4857-5. $16.95 paperback (Canada: $25.95)

Wherever books are sold

Three Rivers Press
Crown Publishing.com